FINDING YOUR WAY

UNDERSTANDING PEOPLE AND WHY THEY DO THE THINGS THEY DO

BY DAVID RUSH

Order this book online at www.trafford.com
or email orders@trafford.com

Most Trafford titles are also available at major online book retailers.

Note for Librarians: A cataloguing record for this book is available from Library
and Archives Canada at www.collectionscanada.ca/amicus/index-e.html

Printed in Victoria, BC, Canada.

ISBN: 978-1-4251-0063-1

*We at Trafford believe that it is the responsibility of us all, as both individuals
and corporations, to make choices that are environmentally and socially sound.
You, in turn, are supporting this responsible conduct each time you purchase a
Trafford book, or make use of our publishing services. To find out how you are
helping, please visit www.trafford.com/responsiblepublishing.html*

*Our mission is to efficiently provide the world's finest, most comprehensive
book publishing service, enabling every author to experience success.
To find out how to publish your book, your way, and have it available
worldwide, visit us online at www.trafford.com/*

Trafford rev. 6/25/2009

 www.trafford.com

North America & international
toll-free: 1 888 232 4444 (USA & Canada)
phone: 250 383 6864 ♦ fax: 250 383 6804 ♦ email: info@trafford.com

Dedication

FOR THIS, THE written expression of my thoughts, feelings, observations and research, I owe a debt of gratitude to Dr. Gad Czudner who introduced me to the study of psychology.

Simply put, he taught me to be aware of the emotional plight of the average person; to observe, listen, extract relevant information, and try to understand that this is not an exact science, but merely the researched opinions of many, highly educated and experienced professionals whose primary interest is correcting the problems people have while coping with everyday occurrences. It does, of course, involve dealing with individuals whose main purpose in life seems to be creating problems where none exist.

Thank you, Dr. Gad, for beginning as my mentor and becoming my friend. I became, through unhappy circumstances, a better person.

Forward

THE ETHICS OF human nature have changed greatly since the days of our forefathers. The most prevalent of these new principles of thought are the hopes we have for the generations to follow and the undeniable need for human change. Such change involves new ways of relating to each other, to ourselves, as well as new methods of resolving human conflicts and the search for the perfect balance of our knowledge and power with wisdom and responsibility. At the heart of our concerns and our human relations are issues of power, the reduction of suffering, and having enough peace and security to allow opportunities for recreation and personal development. We are all seeking and achieving some form of change every moment of our lives; from inhalation and exhalation; from one thought to another, we are each constantly engaged in the dynamic movements of a life in process. We, as human beings, have shown a growing fascination with ourselves and our self-awareness.

The development of our cultures and societies are rooted in individual human conduct and it has become very clear that personal change lies at the heart of collective change. Humans can change, but doing so is much more difficult than most theories will admit. There are also limits to how much and how quickly an individual can change without jeopardizing his or her psychological integrity. (Their sense of self and reality)

As Socrates said; "1 believe that the unexamined life is not worth living and the unlived life is not worth examining." Our attempts to improve ourselves are basically healthy and valuable activities, but we are well advised to appreciate the difference between "knowing" ourselves and "being and becoming ourselves."

Success

To laugh often and much.

To win the respect of intelligent people and the affection of children.

To earn the appreciation of honest critics and endure the betrayal of false friends.

To appreciate beauty and find the best in others.

To leave the world a bit better, whether by a healthy child, a garden patch, or a redeemed social condition.

To know even one life has breathed easier because you have lived.

This is to have succeeded.

Ralph Waldo Emerson

TABLE OF CONTENTS

Chapter 1

Who Do You Want To Be?

WE ALL DAYDREAM from time to time and daydreaming in itself is not a destructive activity. Fantasy is often the mainspring of creativity. As a form of experimentation, free from the constraints of reality, we can give free play to our emotions and ideas, testing them and wondering about them, and then making plans to implement them. Healthy fantasies are spontaneous and flexible, able to roam and move around playfully; all essential prerequisites for creativity.

If you often feel depressed, confused and worried that your life is stuck in a rut that isn't going anywhere but have no idea why it is so unfulfilling, then it is time to re-examine it. No amount of vocational testing will tell a person what kind of work or activity will bring gratification and fulfillment. A productive and satisfying life requires commitment to something we can do well or that offers pleasure. In spite of the fact that we live in a culture that idealizes and worships freedom and self-expression, an alarming number of us are secretly terrified of it. Many people feel uncomfortable without someone or some routine controlling them; they've grown anxious at having to manage their lives on their own.

How do we find "meaning" in life? Personal meaning must be created, not accepted, and the process of creating it requires testing and experimentation. We must find ways to bring our inner selves into harmony with the outer world. Most of us do so through love and work, by discovering partners, projects, or pastimes that will satisfy our needs. Loving and working are the ways we express ourselves. Love and work are the building blocks of a gratifying adult life. They give us meaning and purpose.

You must believe through your true inner self that you deserve all of the gratification and happiness life has to offer. Don't substitute a defensive fantasy for genuine self-assertion. This merely promises protection in love and work and, in personal relationships, this fantasy promises to defend against the intimacy that could lead to engulfment or the pains of abandonment by substituting fantasy relationships with unavailable partners for real relationships.

This defensive fantasy allows you to blame "life" rather than your own problems and you may withdraw into a shell where you can avoid the real problems, remain passive in the face of challenges, and deny the real mess your life may be in. The bottom line is you may give up searching for your true inner self and all that would make you truly happy in exchange for the feeling of never being alone with your real self or experiencing the pain of abandonment.

Although most people have occasional doubts about their identities, their self-worth, and their true happiness, and wonder if they are making the most of their lives, they are not dominated by these feelings. You must retain the capacity to experience a wide range of feelings deeply. These include being happy when good things happen, and disappointed and sad when bad things occur.

What happens to you is important, but what you think about what happens to you is even more important. Imagine you've been having a hard time finding a job that you think will be worthwhile and challenging. You've been moving around for the past ten years; first one job, then another. Then the right one comes along; you've had two interviews and they really liked you. It looks as if you finally have your chance. And then someone else gets the job, for no reason you can see. Situations like this, even if they are less dramatic, happen every day. Life for many people is a constant battle, or at least it seems to be. One thing after another goes wrong. What can we do about it? There are some rules but here's the tricky part. We can't just hear the rules and expect that somehow our life will change. If we have trouble in life, then we must change. When we think about it there is one thing you and I have the most control over and that's our attitude. That's the one thing we can change.

We can't control many of the events in our lives and bad fortune hits us all sooner or later. But we can learn to differentiate. There are nuisances in life and there are serious problems. We can learn that there is one thing we have control over. We are not completely adrift in an angry sea, because we can control our reaction to problems and that very often is enough. Once again, it is not important what happens to us but what we think about what happens to us that determines our lives.

Think how much time and emotional energy we waste each day over trifles; stewing and fretting about things that happen in our lives that have absolutely no importance. We all know people who let their violent emotions surface if they're cut off in traffic, or if the food they order in a restaurant is not exactly right.

We are all the victims of injustice at times, but the more we can control our emotions so that these small disturbances don't get through to us and the more we can keep our equanimity when the trifles happen in our lives, the more free we are. If we pick appropriate emotional responses, life becomes happier, more productive, and more effective.

Vain regret has ruined many lives. Each of us could name several major mistakes that we've made in our lives. The healthy person knows that he can only expect so much from himself. He forgives himself the mistakes he makes and goes on to make a life with the pieces that are left, and the further he gets from his mistake, the less it means to him.

The morbid person destroys himself by constantly reliving his mistake, never forgiving himself. He causes himself and his family and friends much suffering because of his inability to forgive himself and forget the past.

The Inner You

One lesson that life teaches us is that as we grow older, both our fears and our hopes are mostly illusions and are not to be taken too seriously. Time after time we learn that that which we fear the most in life usually never happens. We also learn that if our fears come to pass, the actuality is never quite as bad as the fear we had in the first place. In addition, we were not aware of the strength we have to deal with the difficulty.

On the other hand, our specific hopes usually manage to elude us as well. We must be optimistic about life and what the future holds, but so often, even when our specific dreams come true, we find that we are happy for only a brief period. We must still live with the same discontents and frustrations we had before.

This can happen to all of us in this age when we so often ignore our inner needs and real wants. Many of our hopes do not center on what will bring us real peace of mind, but rather what others tell us will make us rich or beautiful.

It is impossible to have real happiness if you do not accept yourself for what you are. Each of us carries a concept in his mind of what he thinks he is. Usually this concept is a combination of real and imaginary qualities that we think we possess. Our self-concept is what we believe to be true about ourselves. If a person pictures himself as inferior, he acts inferior; or, if he doesn't act inferior, then he may over-compensate by acting arrogant.

A healthy inner self provides for the experience of emotions, both good and bad, and these feelings are a necessary and fundamental part of life. Do not build barriers against these feelings or go into hiding. Accept the wide range of feelings and do not be afraid to express them. This includes the ability to identify your own unique individuality, wishes, dreams, and goals and to be assertive in expressing them autonomously. It also includes taking the necessary steps to make these dreams a reality and supporting and defending them when they are under attack.

You must have the capacity to express yourself fully and honestly in a close relationship with another person with minimal anxiety about abandonment or engulfment. You must also have the capacity to be alone without feeling abandoned. It enables you to manage yourself and your feelings on your own through periods when there is no one special person in your life and to not confuse this type of aloneness with the psychic loneliness. Do not allow yourself to be driven to despair or the pathologic need to fill up your life with meaningless sexual activity or dead-end relationships just to avoid coming face to face with an impaired inner self.

Mind you, not all people with impaired inner selves function poorly. Many are very successful at work. Some with artistic talent find a niche for themselves in such fields as acting, writing, or painting. They may use a high I.Q. and a tendency to intellectualize to enter a profession such as law or medicine. Closer examination will probably reveal that the motivation for the work is not self-expression but meeting the expectations of others. It may also reveal that these people suffer a great deal of anxiety about their achievements and have very unrewarding personal lives.

One of the true tests of the *inner you* is intimacy. It calls for self-expression, self-revelation, and the ability to function independently while sharing with another human being. It requires two people to offer each other affection and acknowledgment in a close, ongoing, personal relationship. It is necessary to perceive the loved one as a complete human being with both good and bad traits; and to be able to feel genuine concern for others; the capacity to tolerate anxiety and depression; and the capacity to commit oneself emotionally to another.

Self-Control Insures Calmness

The following excerpts are from James Allen's book *"As A Man Thinketh"*

"Calmness of mind is one of the beautiful jewels of wisdom. It is the result of long and patient effort in self-control. Its presence is an indication of ripened existence, and of a more than ordinary knowledge of the laws and operations of thought.

A man becomes calm in the measure that he understands himself, for such knowledge necessitates the understanding of others as the result of thought, and as he develops an understanding, and sees more and more clearly the internal relations of things by the action of cause and effect, he ceases to fuss and fume and worry and grieve and remains poised, steadfast and serene.

The calm man, having learned how to govern himself, knows how to adapt himself to others; and they, in turn, feel that they can learn from him and rely on him. The more tranquil a man becomes, the greater is his success, his influence and his power for the good. The strong, calm man is always loved and revered. Who, after all, does not love a tranquil heart; a sweet-tempered, balanced life? That exquisite poise of character which we call serenity is the last lesson of culture and is as precious as wisdom.

How many people do we know who sour their lives, who ruin all that is sweet and beautiful by explosive tempers, who destroy their poise of character. How few people we meet in life who are well balanced, who have that exquisite poise which is characteristic of the finished character."

Most of us have responsibilities that won't allow us to take time off from life and reflect on our inner self to achieve true serenity and peace. We can, however, take a few moments each day when we close the door of our mind to the outside pressures of the world and create a restful and peaceful solitude for ourselves.

There comes a time in our lives when we have to look back and see where we've been. This is when many people come face to face with themselves for the first time. They fail to take this into consideration as they go about their lives and careers. They are always trying to get the edge, trying to sell the other guy short or get the most out of life with the least amount of effort. They are always looking for the shrewdest deal – one where they gain the most and give the least.

Who says you have to win every battle? Only your pride would make you feel this way. An occasional defeat or minor setback can go a long way in keeping your pride in check. And when you deliberately give in instead of winning your point through ruthlessness and stubbornness, you display a certain individual greatness that will eventually give you more satisfaction than victory would have.

Peace of mind is one major goal of the effective and successful person. It is a state of mind wherein you can enjoy whatever little you possess while working actively to improve on that which is yours. There is no greater goal for anyone than wholeheartedness in life. This can only be achieved to the extent that our inner conflicts are resolved.

You must always bear in mind that, although change is an integral part of the process of functioning as a human being, your focus on changing must be directed at yourself. The greatest source of man's frustration and the most formidable barrier to personal peace of mind is the feeling that you must change someone else. Accepting people as they are, right or wrong, is the only path to take to achieve happiness and satisfaction in life.

Chapter 2

Are You A Victim?

ARE YOU SOMEONE who would like to be completely in charge of your own life? Do you automatically do things according to other people's plans? To live your life the way you choose, you have to be a bit rebellious. You have to be willing to stand up for yourself. You might have to be a bit disturbing to those who have a strong interest in controlling your behavior – but if you're willing, you'll find that being your own person, not letting someone else do your thinking for you, is a joyful, worthy, and absolutely fulfilling way to live.

You don't have to be a revolutionary, just a human being who says to the world, and everyone in it, "I am going to be my own person, and resist anyone who tries to stop me."

You must feel strongly enough about not being manipulated by others that you are willing to put a stop to it. You must want your own freedom more than anything else. Often, you must be "insubordinate," to people who would manipulate you. To be anything else is to be victimized, and the world is full of people who would love you to behave in whatever ways are most convenient for them.

Individuals have the right to decide how they will live their lives as long as exercising this right does not infringe on the rights of others. Anyone who interferes with this right must be viewed as a victimizer.

Each person's life is unique, separate from every other life in the world. No one else can live your life, feel what you feel, or experience the world the way you do. This is the only life you get, and it is too precious to let others take their own advantage of it. It is only logical that you should determine how you are going to function, and your functioning ought to bring you joy and fulfillment.

Most people know all too well what it is like to be manipulated, and pushed into behaviors and beliefs against their will. It is almost impossible to victimize people who won't let themselves be victims and who are willing to protest against those who want to subjugate them in any way. If you are being victimized, the problem rests in you, not in all of those other people who have been allowed to control your life.

You need never be a victim again, but in order to function as an individual, you must take a hard look at yourself and learn to recognize the numerous situations in which you are being manipulated for the selfish pleasure of someone else.

What is a victim?

Victims are people who run their lives according to the dictates of others. They find themselves doing things they really would rather not do, or being manipulated into activities loaded with unnecessary personal sacrifice that breeds hidden resentment. But, remember; YOU CAN RARELY BE VICTIMIZED UNLESS YOU ALLOW IT TO HAPPEN.

Victims almost always operate from weakness. They let themselves be dominated, pushed around, because they often feel they are not smart enough or strong enough to be in charge of their lives.

To be free does not mean denying your responsibilities to your loved ones or your fellow man. Indeed, it includes the freedom to make choices to be responsible. But nowhere is it dictated that you must be what others want you to be when their wishes conflict with what you want for yourself. You can be responsible and free. Most of the people who will try to tell you that you cannot or who will label your push for freedom as "selfish," will turn out to have some measure of authority over your life, and they will really be afraid to relinquish the hold they have on you. If they can make you feel selfish, they've contributed to you feeling guilty, and immobilized you once again.

Freedom is not to imply that you should in any way isolate yourself from others. On the contrary, non-victims are most often people who love having fun with others. They carry themselves in an uplifted, gregarious manner, and they are more secure in their relationships because they refuse to let their lives be run by manipulators. They do not need surliness or argumentative stances, because they have learned to feel from within that "this is my life, I experience it alone, and my time here on Earth is very limited. I cannot be owned by anyone else. If you love me, you love me for what I am, not for what you want me to be."

Don't let yourself get caught up in that old, familiar feeling of; "I'll hurt their feelings if I do what I want." This is another tactic that will almost always end up with you doing what other people want you to do and not what you want to do. If others know they can manipulate you by having their feelings hurt, that is precisely what they will do whenever you get out of line or declare your independence. Ninety-five percent of hurt feelings are strategy designed to maintain the control they have over you. People will use their hurt feelings over and over on you if you are gullible enough to buy it. Only victims live their lives on the premise that they must always watch out for others' getting hurt feelings. This is not a license to be obstinately inconsiderate, but simply a basic understanding that people generally stop having hurt feelings when they realize that those feelings can no longer be used to manipulate you.

One of the favorite tactics of the victimizer is to use the phrase "You should have..." A "should have" will not change a thing you've done, but is used to get you to admit that you were wrong, and to avoid dealing with you about what can be done now. As long as the victimizer can keep the focus on your past decisions that didn't turn out well, you may draw the conclusion that you should have asked for and followed your victimizers advice.

When people use the "you should have" tactic, they are usually interested in having you feel bad for your mistakes and convincing you that you aren't capable of making good decisions without their input. It's a common tactic used to keep the focus on what has already happened. Any answer you come up with will generally meet with scorn, disapproval, and a statement that they were right all along, even though they had never given any advice about the situation to begin with.

Another common phrase to keep you retreating is "If you said it before, why don't you mean it now?" This is the "logic of forever," meaning that if it suits their purposes, people will try to hold you to everything you've ever said, even decades later, and even though you may have changed as situations change, you are behaving contrary to what you once said, and this makes you immoral and unethical. If you can be made to feel bad for having changed, then you will very likely revert back and hold yourself accountable for what you originally said, even if you don't mean it now – which will, of course, make your victimizer happy, and effective.

Victimizing Yourself

While others are willing to use past references to manipulate you as they choose, you can also do quite a job on yourself in this regard. Perhaps you, like many others, are living today based on feelings from the past even though they no longer apply. You may even feel trapped by your past, but are unwilling to let go and start fresh.

As you assess past influences on your life, make sure you're not hanging onto the belief that someone else is responsible for what you are feeling today. If you blame your parents or the hard times for your problems of today, keep this sentence in your mind: "If my past is at fault for what I am today, and the past cannot be changed, I am doomed to stay as I am." Today is always a brand new experience, and you can decide now to forget all the unpleasant things you remember from your past and make this moment a pleasant one.

The simple truth about parents is, *They did what they knew how to do. Period.* If your father was an alcoholic, or he abandoned you as an infant; if your mother was overprotective or uncaring, then that is what they knew how to do at the time. Whatever happened to you in your childhood, you have very likely made it more traumatic than it was at the time. Young children usually adapt to anything and they don't go through their days whining or feeling sorry for themselves. They pretty much accept their parents actions and attitudes as they were and they get along. Their heads are filled with the wonder of all things new and they are creatively having a good time, even in the face of what others would call miserable conditions. But in our culture, adults often analyze their pasts repeatedly and remember abusive experiences, many of which never happened.

Keep in mind that any psychological interpretation of your past is simply a professional hunch, which will promote your self-understanding if you believe it to be true. The truth is not in the hunch, but in your being satisfied that it is helpful and correct. While I admit that you can develop insight into yourself by examining your past, the fact is that the insight itself won't change the past or the present, and that blaming your past for what you are today will simply keep you stuck where you are.

Shakespeare alludes to this folly we have of consuming ourselves with the past in lines from several of his plays. One of these is "What's gone and past help, should be past grief." Another is "Things without remedy, should be without regard; what is done, is done."

Here are some questions to ask yourself to determine how effective you are to yourself.

- Do you get upset when you can't get a point across to other people?

- Do you have to announce your accomplishments to others?

- Do you have to tell others whenever you've defeated someone at something?

- Do you find yourself saying or thinking, "He (or she) doesn't understand me."

- Do you explain yourself a lot, and resent having to do so?

If you answered these questions with a "Yes", then you are a victim of yourself. You shouldn't feel that you have to explain yourself to others or make them understand you all the time. You only have to prove your worth to yourself.

Being effective means that you don't have to feel compelled to tell anyone else about your victories to make them meaningful to you. While it is often appropriate to discuss your accomplishments with friends, you shouldn't feel that this is something you have to do before you can be satisfied yourself.

Being effective also means that you don't have to rub your fellow man's face in your victories. If you have to do this, you will find others retaliating, trying to frustrate you in some way. If you have self-confidence, then pleasing yourself will be enough, but, if you lack self-esteem, then you will look to others for validation of your accomplishments. When you have self-confidence, you will not expect everyone to want to hear your stories.

People in marriages, or in families, do not feel free, mostly because they live with the constant expectation of having to prove themselves. A friendship, on the other hand, one that can last a lifetime, is a relationship in which neither person has to prove himself. A friend has no expectations except that you will be yourself. Honesty, after all, is the cornerstone of friendship.

Be a friend to your spouse and to the other members of your family. Remember, if people in your life are not respected, with the guarantees of privacy and the right not to have to prove or explain themselves every moment, the bonds of love and affection get pulled too tight and become a point of stress.

Here are some ways to stop victimizing yourself:

- Stop explaining yourself when you realize that you resent doing so. Remind yourself and others that you are not obligated to explain your personal behavior to anyone and that any explaining you do will be done because you choose to and not to fulfill someone else's expectations of you.

- Stop telling yourself that you are responsible for making people understand you, and tell people that you expect to be misunderstood sometimes, which is only natural. When people tell you they don't understand you, quote the famous Ralph Waldo Emerson line from *Self-Reliance*, "To be great is to be misunderstood."

- When you are in the company of boorish people who you feel are abusing you with their stories, bragging, or pushiness, try excusing yourself, getting up and leaving. Even in such places as restaurants, you can fight the habit of just sitting there and "taking it." Just go for a short walk. You will not only feel better for having exercised some control, but you will also have taught others to stop using these tactics around you.

- Teach people, with your behavior, that you are going to insist on your privacy. Don't spend endless hours demanding to be left along. Just take the time you feel you want for yourself. Do it firmly but gently, and DO IT. Take your walk, your nap, your reading time in your room and don't be seduced into giving up your private time just because others don't understand.

- Stop doing little things you don't enjoy just because other people won't understand. Assert yourself in deciding where your body ends up. It is your body, after all, and you are not obligated to put it in places where is doesn't want or have to be.

Teaching Others How To Treat You

How are you treated by others? Do you find people taking advantage of you, or not respecting you as a person? Do people make plans without asking you and just assume you will go along? Do you find yourself in roles you dislike because everyone else in your life expects you to behave in a certain way?

Well guess what: "You get treated the way you teach people to treat you." If you feel others abuse your rights, then look at your own thinking and behavior, and ask yourself why you have permitted or even encouraged this type of abuse.

You teach others how to treat you on the basis of what you will tolerate. If you simply "take it," and you have been for a long time, then you have sent out the message that you will not resist their abuse. Think back to the very first time your spouse or partner abused you, by raising his voice, getting angry, or hitting you. What he did was to help you become upset.

It is likely that the incident occurred before you were married, had children or the mutual obligations you likely had later. Your future partner's abusive behavior came as a total surprise, since it was the first time he tried it.

Suppose that instead of being shocked, afraid, or tearful, you stood up, looked him in the eye and said, "I don't intend to take this kind of abuse from you. I think of myself as a person with dignity, and I'm not ever going to be pushed around by you or anyone else. Please give yourself a heavy dose of second thoughts before you try something like this again. That's all I intend to say about it, now or ever."

This may seem a little difficult to imagine but the point is, had you reacted from strength and intolerance for abusive behavior right from the very beginning, you would once and for all have taught your partner that you will not indulge such behavior a second time.

If your reaction was different, such as crying, being hurt or insulted, or fearful, you sent out a signal that, although you did not like the way he was treating you, you would take it, and you would let yourself be manipulated emotionally by it.

Chapter 3

The Process Of Change

CHANGING IS A difficult and slow process. Self-help books sometimes make it seem easier than it is but there are some basic assumptions that, once realized, can make the road less difficult.

First: We all have a part of ourselves that wants to be happy and fulfilled. This process is called self-actualization. The process of change involves reawakening this healthy side and giving it hope.

Second: There are several basic "needs" or desires that will lead most of us to be happier if they are satisfied:

- The need to relate and feel connected to other people.

- The need for independence.

- The need for autonomy.

- The need to feel desirable, competent, successful, attractive and worthwhile.

- The need to express what we want and feel to others.

- The need for pleasure or fun.

- The need to help others, to show concern and love.

Third: People can change in very basic ways. Our inherited temperament, along with our early family and peer experiences, create very powerful forces that act against change. However, while these are strong obstacles that make changing difficult, they do not make it impossible.

<u>Fourth:</u> We all have strong tendencies to resist core change. It is highly unlikely that we will change basic emotional traps without making a conscious decision to do so. Most of us operate on automatic pilot, repeating habits, thinking, feeling, relating and doing what we have practiced over our lifetime. These patterns are comfortable and familiar and we are very unlikely to change them unless we make a concerted, deliberate and sustained effort to do so. If we wait for fundamental change to happen on it's own, it almost certainly won't. We are doomed to repeat the mistakes of the past.

<u>Fifth:</u> Most of us have strong inclinations to avoid pain. This is good and bad. The good part is that we gravitate toward experiences that bring us pleasure and gratification. The bad part is that we avoid facing situations that cause us pain, even when confronting them might lead to emotional growth.

It is pointless to escape from our emotional trap without some idea of the direction we would like our life to take. We must discover our natural inclinations; what it is that will make us truly fulfilled and happy. Each person has an innate set of personal preferences and we must set our lives on a path that will include interests, relationships and activities that will lead us to feel fulfilled.

Our best guide to recognizing natural inclinations is our emotional and bodily sensations. When we engage in activities that fulfill our natural inclinations, we feel good. There are five recognized components to consider when preparing yourself to improve yourself and your life.

- The First Area of Change Involves Relationships.

  Ask yourself what you want from an intimate relationship.

How important is emotional closeness to you compared to sexual excitement? Relationships are almost always a trade-off. Making intelligent trade-offs is a problem for many of us because we are out of touch with our natural inclinations. Very few of us ever find a partner who provides us with everything we need, so we have to make choices. What is most important to you in choosing a partner? What are the less important qualities that would be nice, but which you would do without if you had to?

- The Second Area of Change is Autonomy.

What is the optimal level of independence for you? Naturally, you want to live in a world with a sense of independence, competence, and a strong sense of self. But what balance of autonomy and connection will make you happiest? Autonomy gives you the freedom to seek out healthy relationships and to avoid or leave unhealthy ones. You are free to stay in a relationship because you want to stay, not because you need to. Autonomy is a vital component in the pursuit of your natural inclinations. It involves developing a sense of identity.

- The Third Component of Change is Self-esteem.

Like autonomy, self-esteem provides a context of freedom. Instead of being blocked, you are free. You get to choose a life that enhances your self-esteem.

- The Fourth Component of Change is Self-Assertion.

This involves asking to have your own needs met and expressing your feelings. Asserting yourself allows you to follow your natural inclinations and get pleasure out of life. Passion, creativity, playfulness and fun can help make life worth living. It is important to be able to let go sometimes, to include excitement and pleasure in your life.

- The Fifth Area of Change is Concern for Others.

  One of the most gratifying aspects of life is learning to give to other people and empathizing with them. It feels good to make a contribution. It's important to involve yourself in things that help others: making a connection to something greater that yourself and your individual life.

To begin the road to change you must first be honest with yourself and place a high value on facing reality. To become the person you want to be you must understand the person you are now. It's a difficult realization to acknowledge character flaws but they are present in all of us. The way you treat others is like a mirror into the soul.

The life tasks that we must master to achieve emotional stability and happiness are:

- Friendship (relating to others)

- Work (making a contribution)

- Love (achieving intimacy and family relationships)

- Self-Acceptance (getting along with ourselves)

- Values (life goals, morals, beliefs)

People are free to choose among alternatives and therefore have a large role in shaping their destinies. Because of this we must accept the responsibility for directing our lives. It is possible, however, to avoid this reality by making excuses.

The absolute root cause of most psychological problems is blame. We blame others consistently for events that happen in our lives. We blame friends, parents, authorities, or in some cases, we blame ourselves, but it all relates to *BLAME.* If we are to recover from a personality disorder, we had better learn to stop blaming ourselves and others. We must learn to accept ourselves despite our imperfections. Because we largely create our own disturbed thoughts and feelings, we have the power to control or correct them.

In order to achieve self-awareness there are some factors that we must accept.

- We are finite; we do not have an unlimited time to do what we want with our lives.

- We have the potential to take action or not to act: inaction is a decision.

- We choose our actions, and therefore create our own destinies.

- The meaning of our own life is not automatically bestowed on us but is the product of searching and discovering a unique purpose.

- We are all subject to loneliness, meaninglessness, emptiness, guilt and isolation.

- We are basically alone, yet we have an opportunity to relate to others.

The basic reality is that people contribute to their own psychological problems by the way they interpret events and situations in their lives. Humans are self-evaluating and self-sustaining. They develop emotional and behavioral difficulties when they take simple preferences (desires for love, approval, success) and make the mistake of thinking of them as dire needs.

Chapter 4

WHY CRITICS CRITICIZE

NATURAL LEADERS HAVE the subtle ability to guide, inspire and motivate others without demands, orders or criticism. Critical, domineering attitudes are dangerous traits to the individual who possesses them. These characteristics almost always create dissension and resentment and yet the person possessing them has no control over his need to use them to assert his assumed, superior position in any given situation.

Criticism, for example, is one of the many tools parents use to control children. It's use is mostly prevalent in situations where the one trying to assert control is of a lower than average intellectual capacity and therefore must resort to the basic means of trying to get others to obey him. Criticism is usually followed by threats of punishment, but never earns respect. It only generates feelings of anxiety, hurt and isolation. If we have endured this type of verbal assault, we carry with us the message that criticism means we have been bad or that we are inadequate. We rarely internalize the fact that criticism is nothing more than a string of words that hurt, usually spoken by someone who feels that demeaning others is the surest and only way they can raise their own self-esteem.

There are many reasons for a person to try and exert his will on others using the criticism tactic. Some of the intentions are to:

- To dominate and control

- To get attention

- To manipulate

- To protect their own self interest

- To project their own faults on to you

- To change you (even if you don't want to change)

- To punish or get even

- To distract you from an issue that is sensitive to them

- To show you who's the boss

The four main responses to criticism are:

- Defense

- Denial

- Counterattack

- Withdraw

Why do we persistently respond to criticism in these ways? We learned these responses when we were very young. With years of practice, we have gotten very good at these responses until they have become habit. Unfortunately, they are bad habits. Continual defense or denying can lead our critics to suspect that we truly are guilty of something. And it can lead us to feel guilty even when we've done nothing wrong.

Defense

If your response to criticism is to defend yourself, you definitely have a low self-esteem problem. Most times when the defense emerges instinctively, you probably aren't even sure what you have done wrong but are willing to accept the responsibility simply because you are being told that you are wrong and deserve punishment.

Denial

This is a pitiful and weak response to criticism. Phrases like 'I'm sorry, I didn't mean it', are commonplace in this response. We are willing to accept the criticism in order to keep the peace. We may even assume that what we have done or said is wrong simply because it displeases someone else. Self-assertion is an integral part of healthy self-esteem. Every person has the right to their own opinion in any situation and the right to express it providing it doesn't intentionally hurt someone else unnecessarily.

Counterattack

When we counterattack, our emotions are heightened and our rational thinking grinds to a halt. All of our hard-won communication skills fly out the window when we fly off the handle. Counterattacking may temporarily slow down the hail of criticism but it blocks communication, builds resentment, and often leads to more aggressive tactics by the criticizing party.

Withdraw

The last of the common defenses is to withdraw. Victims of criticism withdraw when it's easier to accommodate than to continue to press for a chance to get a word in. They've learned that passive behavior brings peace, even if it does damage to their sense of personal power and self-esteem. Very often, our opinions have a great deal of merit but if we keep them and our feelings to ourselves to promote peace and harmony, we not only prevent our personal growth but hinder our effectiveness in our relationships and our lives.

Why Do They Do It?

To Dominate And Control – People who use criticism to dominate you want to put themselves in a commanding position. They want to stand above you and enhance their own power by putting you on the defensive. Not everyone who is dominant is controlling, however. Many people have the stature, charisma, and abilities that make them natural leaders, but their dominance is based on the way they present themselves and the work they do, not on the ability to keep others down.

In fact, many people are dominant because they have the gift of bringing out the best in others. But beware of people who use their strength and forcefulness to intimidate you and push their ideas on you. Their critical behavior is meant to enhance their own position, not to help you. Controlling people often use criticism to keep the world running their way. They don't criticize to help others or improve relationships, but to ensure that things are done the "right way", that is, their way. To these people, the appearance of success is very important. And on the surface, things usually look fine. If they looked deeper into themselves, however, (which they generally won't do), they would find that they lack real friends and real respect. Because they refuse to listen, other people find it difficult to be honest with them. Their long-term relationships generally erode because these abrasive, difficult controllers lack the capacity to listen to and accept criticism about their negative impact on others. Their controlling behavior is the source of their security and power. It is extremely crucial to your self-esteem to stand up to this type of person and not allow yourself to be run over emotionally by them.

To Manipulate – Manipulators use criticism to induce guilt in others. They often use terms such as "you never" or "you always" or "so and so does this and you don't". Manipulators want to get their own way, but they don't use a simple, direct, adult mode of communication to get it.

To Abuse – Abuse occurs when one person controls or subjugates another through humiliation, fear, intimidation, and physical or verbal assaults. People don't have to use their fists to abuse one another. Words and mood swings are powerful weapons. Any relationship in which attacks are sharp, venomous and personal is abusive. An abuser will denigrate his partner's abilities, whether it be to clean the kitchen counter or to succeed in their job. He will challenge his partner's opinions about politics, philosophy or even religion calling them stupid if they did not agree with his opinion. Bear in mind that the abuser can be as charming and loving one day as he can be nasty and abusive the next day.

To Change You –Changers are not satisfied with you and who you are and want to change you, even if you don't need or want to change. They tell you to act differently, to think differently; they want you to conform to their image of you.

To Show You Who's The Boss – Some people use criticism to establish and maintain a superior position in the relationship. They try to get you to defend yourself and answer to them, so that it is clear to everyone involved – "who's the boss".

To Get Their Own Way – Some people become harsh critics the second they suspect that they are not going to get exactly what they want exactly when they want it. They tend to be spoiled, intolerant people who believe that they are entitled to have everything their own way.

Dealing With Criticism

The most effective initial response to a critic's words is silent observation. It gives you time to distance yourself from the criticism and get your thoughts and feelings into balance. Pay particular attention to judgment words like passive, stupid, lazy, selfish, disorganized, etc. These words do not reflect reality. Behavior reflects reality. Subjective words reflect the speaker's opinion, nothing more. Just because someone interprets a particular behavior as bad or wrong does not make it so. That is simply one person's opinion.

As you observe, you will find that your feelings are not so easily triggered by criticism. The process of observing allows you to objectify and distance yourself. You will be thinking more and feeling less. This is one way of overcoming the negative emotions attached to criticism and will allow you to be more in control.

Has anyone ever told you they were just giving you some "constructive criticism?" Just how constructive is "constructive criticism," anyway? Often it isn't helpful nor is it meant to be. Many times it is intended to intimidate, ridicule, or diminish the person to whom it is directed, usually motivated by the critic's need to bolster their own weakening self-esteem. You may have noticed that extremely intelligent people don't seem to spend a lot of time explaining people's faults to them.

When we criticize people in an inconsiderate manner, we create unpleasant feelings. Since these feelings are so unpleasant, it's only natural to try to escape from someone who is habitually critical.

A large part of the critics purpose is to keep his victim on the defensive. Most critics don't want their own behavior to be scrutinized too closely and one way to accomplish this is to keep people in the position of defending themselves.

A good stance to take in life is to walk away and stay away from anyone who is making it their life's work finding fault with everyone they encounter.

Chapter 5

EMOTIONAL TRAUMA

ONE OF THE downsides of letting your emotions have a say in your life is the devastation you may fall victim to when forces outside of your control blindside you with pain, heartache and worry. This can be caused by one or more of the following stressful life events:

- Death of a spouse, child, or someone equally close to you

- Divorce

- Incarceration

- Loss of a job

- Serious personal illness

Each of these life events is traumatic and requires a major adjustment because each causes us to lose something important: security, love, freedom or self-esteem. If you have suffered a loss such as these, you may have asked yourself questions like:

- "Why me?"

- "What did I do to deserve this?"

- "Will my life ever be normal again?"

- "Is this just a bad dream?"

- "How long can I take this?"

If so, you can be certain that you have experienced a traumatic, life-altering change. The painful emotions and haunting questions you asked yourself on this, the worst day of your life, were actually signals that whatever happened to you has robbed you of the resources that were critical to your intellect. The event may have obliterated some of your intimate ties; it may have destroyed your career path or taken away your financial security; or it may have damaged you mentally or physically. In short, you lost your inner balance.

A study by Dr. Stevan Hobfoll, director of the Applied Psychology Center at Kent State University, reveals that traumas involving loss of vital resources for health and happiness are the most psychologically threatening. His contention is substantiated by the fact that stressful loss is responsible for ninety percent of situational depressions.

There are always indicators that can warn you of a trauma-induced disturbance of the communication between your nervous system and other parts of your brain that are responsible for thinking, learning, and memory. Some of the psychological signals are:

- Feeling of being in a daze

- Distractibility and inability to concentrate

- Memory failure

- Preoccupation with the past

- Preoccupation with what might have been

- Daydreaming

- Nightmares

- Rumination over loss

Some of the physiological signals are:

- Chronic fatigue

- Extreme sweating

- Accelerated heart rate

- Digestive disorders

- Sleep disturbances

- Lethargy

You must learn to adapt to the changes in your present and future caused as a result of the trauma. If you don't, you will spend your future dwelling on the past and wishing you could correct or undo whatever happened to you. You cannot travel back in time and the forward passage of time is uncontrollable. This is not to say you should try to 'make the best of it.' You should, in fact, do better that that. There's an old adage that states: "The best revenge is living well." After all, revenge is what you will want at this point. Whatever caused your life change will likely inspire your anger, even if it wasn't a specific person. It may have been a set of unfortunate and unforeseen events or circumstances.

Anger is a signal that we should listen to. Our anger may be a message that we are being hurt, that our rights are being violated, that our needs or wants are not being adequately met, or simply that something is not right. Our anger may tell us that we are not addressing an important emotional issue in our lives or that too much of our self-beliefs, values or ambitions are being compromised in a relationship.

If you find that you are disturbed and confused about life in general when traumatic things happen, most likely it is because you are in the first stage of coping with a crisis of some kind. In addition to the immediate sense of loss and disappointment, you are reminded that you are mortal. The underlying emotional source of all suffering is mortality itself. After all, if your life is altered so dramatically by trauma that you can hardly recognize it as your own, you might naturally think of it as a 'death experience'. In a small but real way, life as you once knew it has died. This small but real death is certainly reminiscent of the ultimate of all traumas – your own death.

Most people spend their lives in pursuit of such positive desires as safety, belonging, respect, prestige and love. When these pursuits seem to elude us, we feel a level of sadness and frustration over the loss of control over our lives. This sadness should not be ignored nor should the emotional pain associated with it. Sadness almost always presents challenges to be met and creates a tenderness of emotions that is essential to being a caring and empathetic person.

Suppose, for example, you were exposed to a child who had lived his life being subjected to regular abuse and deprivation. Would this experience not make you more caring to children in all situations, especially those who had not been treated fairly in life? A person must experience emotional pain in order to understand how it makes others feel.

Emotional pain is seldom as excruciating as that which accompanies the loss of someone we love. When the loss is unexpected, it hurts even more.

Diversion

What you must avoid in all circumstances of unresolved stress is the emotional strategy of 'Diversion'. What this entails is the complete ignoring of the trauma and the pain caused by the stress associated with the problem. When you do this, you will have a tendency to withdraw completely from any situations which contain the possibility of exposing you to another trauma or painful episode. You will basically end up living as an emotional recluse, refusing to be involved in any situations where you will meet new people, have relationships that could end, or taking risks that could end up with a bad result.

The kind of life that this would allow you to lead would be very unfulfilling and, although offer no potential for pain, neither would it allow opportunities for happiness, adventure, or great success in your future.

Chapter 6

Emotional Traps

EMOTIONAL TRAPS ARE patterns of thought and behavior that begin as a result of trauma, childhood experiences, or emotional damage caused at some point in your life. They may last forever unless you learn how to recognize them and the problems they can cause. These traps can determine how we think, feel, act and relate to others. They trigger such strong feelings as anger, sadness and anxiety and can inhibit your ability to savor and enjoy life to its fullest.

To determine whether you are caught in an emotional trap, ask yourself the following questions:

- Do you find yourself clinging to people you're close to because you are afraid they will leave you?

- Are you usually on the lookout for people's ulterior motives because you don't trust people easily?

- Do you feel that you can't cope well by yourself, so you feel the need for other people to help you get by?

- Do you feel like you don't belong; that you are different and don't really fit in?

- Do you feel that if someone knew the real you, with all your defects exposed, they couldn't possibly care for you?

- Do you feel ashamed of yourself; unworthy of the love, attention and respect of others?

- Do you feel inadequate because you don't measure up to others in terms of talent, intelligence, or success?

- Do you feel you have no choice but to give in to other people's wishes; otherwise they will retaliate or reject you in some way?

- Do people see you as doing too much for others and not enough for yourself?

If any or all of these statements apply to you, you may be caught in one of the emotional traps I will describe to you in the following pages. If this is the case and you make yourself aware of it, you can take the first steps to changing your thoughts, feelings and life for the better. You must understand three very important characteristics of emotional traps.

1. They may last for your whole life.

2. They are self-destructive.

3. They will struggle for survival.

Abandonment

This is the feeling that the people you love will leave you and you will end up emotionally isolated forever. Whether you feel that these people will die, find someone new, or simply leave you forever, you feel that you will be left alone. Because of this feeling, you cling to people close to you too much. Ironically, by doing this, you end up pushing them away. You become abnormally upset or angry over even normal separations. You have difficulty tolerating any withdrawal in a relationship. You worry about even relatively small changes, exaggerating the probability that the relationship will end.

The slightest sign of dissatisfaction from your partner appears to you to be evidence that they want to end the relationship. Jealousy and possessiveness are common themes. Your relationships are marked by frequent breakups and tumultuous reconciliation's. You seem to be attracted to partners who are emotionally unstable or ambivalent about you. One moment they act deeply in love with you and the next moment they act as though you do not exist.

Many people in this trap often have a number of people lined up as backup in case their main person leaves. They have someone immediately available to take the person's place, or they find someone new, and quickly form another dependent relationship. Most people caught in this trap are quite talented at finding someone to take care of them and they go from one person to another with rarely more than a month in between.

This is not necessarily true of people who fear emotional abandonment. They can be alone for long periods of time. They might withdraw from close relationships out of hurt and out of fear of being hurt again. They have already faced the loneliness and they know that they can survive. It is the process of loss that is devastating. It is having that connection, and then losing it, and being thrown back into the loneliness once again. Some people cope by avoiding intimate relationships altogether. They would rather remain alone than go through the process of loss again.

Even though you may have experienced a lot of abandonment in your life, in a lot of ways this may be because you have been most attracted to partners who have trouble making commitments. These are the exact people to whom you are usually most attracted. I'm not saying that you should go out with people you find unattractive, but an intense sexual attraction may be a sign that your partner is triggering your 'Abandonment Emotional Trap'. If this is so, the relationship means trouble, and you should probably think twice before pursuing it. People in your life don't have to be like that. You can eliminate the people who are like that from your life and choose to associate with people who are able to be there for you and make a commitment.

Mistrust And Abuse

This is the expectation that people will hurt or abuse you in some way; that they will cheat, lie to you, manipulate, humiliate, physically harm, or otherwise take advantage of you. If you are caught in this trap, you hide behind a wall of mistrust to protect yourself. You never let people get too close. You expect that the people you love will betray you. Either you avoid relationships altogether, form superficial relationships, or you form relationships with people who treat you badly and then feel angry and vengeful towards them.

Dependence

If you are caught in the dependence trap, you feel unable to handle everyday life in a competent manner without help from others. You depend on others to act as a crutch and need constant support. You seek out strong figures upon whom to become dependent and allow them to rule your life.

Social Exclusion

Social exclusion involves your connection to friends and groups. You feel isolated from the rest of the world and socially undesirable. These feelings may not become apparent in one-on-one situations and it surprises you to realize how anxious and aloof you may feel at parties, classes, meetings or social gatherings.

Defectiveness

This emotional trap relates directly to your self-esteem. You feel inwardly flawed and defective. You believe that you would be fundamentally unlovable to anyone who got close enough to really know you. You find it difficult to believe that people close to you value you, so you expect rejection. Ask yourself if any of the following statements apply to you:

- No one could love me if they really knew me.

- I have secrets that I do not want to share, even with the people closest to me.

- I hide the real me. The real me is unacceptable. The self I show is a false self.

- I am often critical and reject others, especially people who seem to love me.

- I devalue my positive qualities.

- I live with a great deal of shame about myself.

- One of my greatest fears is that my faults will be exposed.

If you experience one or many of these feelings regularly, you may be caught in the 'Defectiveness Emotional Trap'. The emotion that is most connected to this trap is shame. Shame is what you feel when your defects are exposed. You will do almost anything to keep your defectiveness hidden.

You feel that your defectiveness is inside you. It is not immediately observable. Rather, it is something in the essence of your being. You feel completely unworthy of love. This is one of the most common emotional traps, but it is often hard to detect. Because your imagined defect is internal, you suffer even more from the terror of being exposed.

If you are caught in this trap you may experience a chronic, vague unhappiness without being able to explain why. You don't realize that your depression is a result of your negative view of yourself. Feeling unworthy and angry at yourself is a large part of depression. You may feel that you have been depressed your whole life; a kind of low level depression lurking in the background. If your primary style of coping is to escape, you may have addictions or compulsions. Drinking, drugs, overworking and overeating are all ways of numbing yourself to avoid the pain of feeling worthless. It is very important to realize that the Defectiveness Emotional Trap is not usually based on a real defect but rather how you are made to feel about yourself.

A method of dealing with this trap is to pace how much you reveal of yourself when considering opening up to someone. As you become more intimate and sense that your partner seems to genuinely care for you, you can disclose more and more. It can be a risk to expose everything all at once. If you have secrets; humiliating things that happened to you; gradually tell them to people close to you. There is an expression; "You are only as bad as your worst secret". Many things that we hide from people are not as bad as we think. Once we share them with someone, we see that they are not so shameful. We see that the person still loves us, and we feel better about ourselves.

Subjugation

If you are caught in this emotional trap, you sacrifice your own needs and desires for the sake of pleasing others or meeting their needs. You allow others to control you, either out of guilt; that you will hurt other people by putting yourself first; or fear that you will be punished or abandoned if you disobey. You repeatedly enter relationships with dominant, controlling people and subjugate yourself to them or you enter relationships with needy people who are too damaged to give back to you in return.

Basically, you experience the world in terms of control issues.

Other people in your life always seem to be in control; you feel controlled by the people around you. At the core of your subjugation is the conviction that you must please others. In all likelihood, there is one exception to your rule of pleasing; the only person you do not feel obliged to please is yourself. It is what the other person wants that comes first.

You feel trapped by circumstances or swept along by fate. Rather than an actor, you are a reactor. You feel that there is little you can do to solve your problems. You merely wait and hope that suddenly, everything will get better.

You probably think of yourself as the kind of person with whom it is easy to get along. Since you are so agreeable and eager to please, and tend to avoid conflict, naturally you get along with others. You see yourself as someone who is willing to accommodate. You might even consider this one of your assets; that you are flexible and able to adjust to many types of people. But, you have difficulty setting limits on the demands other people make of you. When people ask you to do things that are unreasonable, such as more than your share of work, you say "yes". And you find it extremely difficult to ask others to change their behavior, no matter how much their behavior disturbs you.

Similarly, you might feel proud that you are able to serve others; that you are able to help other people and be attentive to their needs. And you are right. The ability to be there for other people is a strength of self-sacrificing people. You probably have developed exemplary skills in helping others, and may be in one of the helping professions. However, one of your weaknesses is that what you want often gets lost. Too often you are unassertive and silent about your needs.

Your subjugation lowers your self-esteem. You do not feel entitled to the legitimate rights of all people in relationships. Everyone has rights except you. Because you lack a strong sense of self, of who you are, there is the danger that you might lose yourself in your subjugator. You can become so immersed in trying to meet the needs of other people that you begin to blend or merge into these people. The boundary between who you are and who they are becomes blurred. You might adopt other people's goals and opinions as your own.

If you have any chance to escape from this trap, there are certain characteristics you must avoid in potential partners. Here are some of the danger signals that can help you avoid the pain of the subjugation emotional trap:

- People who are domineering and constantly expect to have things their own way.

- People who become irritated or angry when you disagree with them or attend to your own needs.

- People who pout or pull away from you when you do things your own way.

- People who try to make you feel guilty or accuse you of being selfish when you ask to do something your way.

- People with whom you have to carefully watch what you say or do because they have a bad temper.

Becoming involved with partners who demonstrate these traits is a sure path to emotional self-destruction and usually these are the people you will feel the most attracted to because you have a low self-esteem and can fall very easily into the martyr pattern wherein you will most certainly have the pity of those who know you best. You will often hear phrases such as; "You must be a Saint to put up with that".

Remember that your Subjugation Trap has the strength of a lifetime of memories and a multitude of repetitions and confirmations that are right. Your subjugation feels right to you and is central to your entire self-image and view of the world. You find comfort and reassurance in holding onto this trap, regardless of its negative consequences for your life.

Entitlement

This trap is associated with the inability to accept other people's opinion of what is reasonable. When you want something, you want it immediately. You have no tolerance or patience with what you require of others and this costs you dearly in the lack of respect you will incur as a result of your demands. You usually become very angry when you don't get what you want.

Any of these emotional traps will struggle for survival and you will feel a strong need to maintain it. This is a part of the basic human drive for consistency. The trap we live in is what we know. Although it is painful and self-destructive, it is comfortable and familiar. It is therefore very difficult to escape from. Different people cope with emotional traps in different ways. This explains why children raised in the same environment can appear to be so different. This is partly because we have different temperaments at birth and our temperaments push us in certain directions.

When you suffer from the 'Entitlement Emotional Trap' you have little empathy or concern for the feelings of others. This leads you to be inconsiderate or perhaps abusive. You believe that although other people should be punished when they violate social norms, you should not be punished. You do not expect to have to pay the normal consequences for your actions. You may have a tendency to procrastinate. When you finally do the task, you do it half-heartedly or passive-aggressively. You just cannot get yourself to focus and persevere. Even when you want to stick to something it is hard for you.

You may have trouble controlling your emotions, particularly anger. Although you may have some depression, anger is your predominant emotion. You are not able to express your anger in a mature way. Rather, you are like an enraged child. You become impatient, irritable and angry.

You are self-indulgent about expressing your anger. You feel that you should be free to vent any emotion. You never consider the impact this has on other people. Unlike many of the other traps which cause people to suppress their needs, the Entitlement Emotional Trap involves the excessive expression of your needs. You lack a normal degree of restraint. Whereas other people inhibit and discipline themselves appropriately, you do not.

Your life becomes painful only when you are no longer able to avoid the serious negative consequences that result from your actions. For example, you lose your family or partner because you are too moody, difficult to please, or angry when you do not get your own way, which, by your opinion, is the only proper way. Only then will you acknowledge that other people are not happy with your behavior and that you have a problem.

You are attracted to partners who:

- Sacrifice their own needs for yours.

- Allow you to control them.

- Are afraid to express their own needs and feelings.

- Are willing to tolerate abuse and lack of respect.

- Allow you to take advantage of them.

- Do not have a strong sense of self and allow themselves to live through you.

Here are some of the signs that you may be caught in this Emotional Trap.

- You do not care about the needs of other people around you.

- You get your needs met at their expense.

- You may humiliate or demean people around you.

- You may have difficulty empathizing with the feelings of those around you.

- Your partner, family, friends, or children may leave you, resent you, or limit contact with you because you treat them unfairly.

- You never have a chance to experience the joy of having a truly equal, reciprocal relationship.

- You never allow yourself to face and solve your underlying emotional problems. Your real needs are never addressed.

- You infringe on the rights of people close to you to use their own time for themselves.

- Your demands become a drain on the people around you.

- People you need may eventually become fed up or angry with your demands on them and leave you.

People with the 'Entitlement Emotional Trap' rarely want to change. They do not read self-help books. They resist going to therapy. Instead, they blame others for their problems and fight to stay the same.

Chapter 7

Behavior At Work (Social Harmony)

A RECENT COUNTRY-WIDE survey evaluated the 50 best companies to work for in Canada. This survey sent invitations to more than 1500 companies, each with over 300 employees, to participate in the survey.

The top companies did not represent glamorous, high-paying dream jobs. According to the thousands of employees who responded to the survey, the top 50 companies were chosen for their focus on the details of daily work and operations. These day-to-day details make the real, tangible and positive difference in attitude and culture for a company's staff.

According to the survey, the following criteria are what made employees feel their company is a good place to work.

Communication

Honest and open communication plays a key role. Top managers at the best companies communicate more often and more effectively with employees. As a result, employees identify more closely with management and its goals.

Recognition

Corporate attitude also separated the best companies from the rest. The top-rated companies foster the small business mentality. These companies make their employees feel important and offered their people praise, which made them feel a sense of importance to the system. Organizations that ranked high on the survey articulate a clear and concise vision, as well as developing programs to keep staff focused on their goals and actually listening to their suggestions and concerns.

Some companies spend millions of dollars to ensure that their employees are better paid, when, in fact, money can play a minor role in motivating staff. Yes, employees care about salaries and benefits, but it's the total package that the company offers that matters the most.

Good employees, after all, are a company's best investment. Taking the time to make sure your company has invested in its environment and ultimately its reputation attracts top talent employees.

When making business decisions about people you work with on a daily basis, emotional intelligence must be a key factor. You must be able to identify with and feel empathy for the effect your decisions will have on others. The trick is not to emphasize your own feelings over the other person's problems. That's sympathy. Empathy is discovering and experiencing inside yourself how these problems feel to the other person.

Social harmony is crucial to the success of a business venture which requires the time and effort of people other than yourself. All businesses tend to have a top performer; a "superstar", so to speak. When there is constant disharmony in the workplace, the best workers will not work to their highest potential. Social disruption is a serious deterrent to high production levels. When there is frequent tension, workers tend to become tired more easily and de-motivated to give their all. They feel no satisfaction from a 'job well done'.

Of course, there will always be the negative people in any situation, but when the majority of employees feel good about the job they do and are happy with their co-workers, the disrupters will, sooner or later, feel out of place and out-numbered. They will witness, first hand, the good feeling the others have about their tasks and the hours they put in doing the best job they can.

Disharmony must be dealt with as soon as it becomes apparent and people's personal or work problems must be treated as genuine and serious. The employee or co-worker will feel that if you don't treat their concerns as legitimate, then you probably don't care about them as people.

The word *empathy* is used more and more in business and family life. The dictionary defines empathy as the capacity to participate in another person's feelings or ideas; that is, to put yourself in the other fellow's shoes. Empathy is not sympathy. It's entirely possible to sympathize with a person without ever feeling empathy for them. You may commiserate with their problem, and yet have no idea what they are really feeling. You may even want to help them and yet never share their feelings.

The ability to place yourself in another person's position is a quality that can be developed. It can lead to success in many areas of human relations. It's easy to go through life ignoring the needs and feelings of the other person. We so often say, "I know what you mean," but seldom do we really know what the other person means because we don't take his needs, wants, and desires into consideration. Other people can be just as cold as we are. Only a small portion of them is revealed in what they tell us. If we can develop a habit of hearing not only what is said, but sensing what someone really feels, we can improve our business and family relations immeasurably. We also have to devote a certain amount of time and energy dealing with people we like and ones we dislike. We can't underestimate the value of any individual we may deal with.

There are many situations where a newer employee is appointed as a manager or supervisor over long term and experienced people. The good leaders don't bluff or pull rank. They admit that there is a lot they don't know. They assume responsibility firmly, but are quick to admit they need help. The good manager knows that you get things done through people, and not in spite of them.

There is only one way to achieve most goals, and that is by working with and through other people. It's a hard thing to admit when you think how exasperating we can all be, but it's the truth.

Perhaps the greatest of all businessmen is J. Paul Getty. Here is what he said about how he made his first billion: "It doesn't make much difference how much other knowledge or experience an executive possesses; if he is unable to achieve results through people, he is worthless as a manager."

If you are in a situation where you must have a confrontation with someone, settle for simple victory. Don't be the kind of person who humiliates someone. It's a matter of discretion; and determining how far to go in handling a given situation is difficult, to say the least. There is no set formula to help us. We have to be able to evaluate each encounter and make our own determination of how far to go.

Some people are liked by nearly everyone; others can't seem to get along with anybody. How does this come about? What makes people like or dislike us?

Interpersonal behavior is a psychological term that describes how we act in order to get along with others. For example, when you smile at someone, that person is likely to smile in return. Of course, there are many requirements for achieving healthy interpersonal relationships, but there is a simple, three-step formula which can help.

- We must act as we really are.

- How we act must please us personally.

- Our actions must be acceptable to others.

The same is usually true in business. When you're the boss, it may be necessary to criticize those who work for you, but you should also remember that often you can turn an inefficient employee into a good worker if you take the time to express your true feelings of satisfaction when they do something that helps the business. Life is difficult. People often need all the encouragement they can get. A kind word can help them face the inevitable trials and hardships of living.

Attitude In The Workplace Is Everything

One of the most complimentary things a boss can say about an employee is "I like their attitude." This one phrase is probably responsible for most of the promotions in business and industry. If that sounds farfetched, consider it for a moment.

What does it take to get ahead? Of course, it takes talent, skill, hard work, and sometimes, a good break. But a poor attitude can undermine all these things. What good are talent, skill, and hard work if they are misapplied?

Nothing can stop the person with the right mental attitude from achieving their goal; and nothing on earth can help the person with the wrong mental attitude. Look around your office and spot the attitudes of the people you work with. There's probably someone who constantly complains that they aren't paid enough. And there's probably someone who complains that they are doing all the work, but nearby, you find someone else doing more work, and doing it cheerfully. The person who says they can run the place better than the boss will probably never get the chance because of their antagonistic attitude.

Vince Lombardi, the great coach of the Green Bay Packers, said that winning is 75 percent mental. Talk with almost any successful person and they will tell you the same thing. Yet how many of us actually apply that to our own lives.

Five Questions To Ask Yourself About Your Job

1. Are your complaints based on real issues or do they reflect insecurity? (Complaints can be a defense mechanism and hide weaknesses in the complainer. People who lack ambition are prone to complain to cover this fact. A person's complaints can also reflect a poor concept of themselves and their abilities.)

2. Do you agree with the objectives of your organization? (If you can't say yes to this, then you are probably with the wrong company. You must agree with the objectives if you are to be an important member of the team.)

3. Do you consider your supervisors fair? (Many times the individual who complains about their supervisors is objecting to the workload placed on them. Supervisors are paid to demand a certain amount of work from the employees in return for a certain amount of pay.)

4. Do you speak well of your organization and defend it when others criticize it? (The valued employee is one who can recognize the good points of an organization along with the bad.)

5. Are you proud to be with the organization? (If you can't take pride in your organization, then there is a chance you will not take pride in your work.)

Your response to these five questions indicates your overall attitude towards the people for whom you work. It tells whether you are the right man or woman for your company and, perhaps more importantly, whether your company is right for you. And you can be sure that your supervisors will ask themselves these questions when they consider you for a raise or a promotion.

Is Skill Enough?

Most of us know how to go about getting a job, but keeping one is another matter. Many people who lose jobs have all the ability and knowledge they need, but quit because of mounting pressures or are fired for the good of the company.

Let's examine some of the reasons other than lack of performance that can cost a person their job. Any supervisor will tell you that by far the most frequent cause of firing is inability to get along with people. Nobody, no matter how capable, will keep a job very long if they are constantly at odds with their fellow workers, resisting instruction and ignoring suggestions. There is no room in a successful corporation for the person who makes everyone their enemy.

Another reason for being fired is inability to exercise self-discipline. Most people get along with others when things are going right. But when the pressure is on, some people fall behind and become hostile and nervous. They are blinded by the urgency of the situation and cannot use the skills they possess to confront and solve the problem. The most valuable person in the company is the one who produces when the heat is on.

A common reason for losing your job is the inability to perform without constant and excessive supervision. The person who runs to the boss with all sorts of trivial problems may have a poor self-concept. They have the skills required to perform the job but are afraid of making a mistake.

Being Indispensable

Our economic system allows people to go as far as their individual initiative will take them. They are free to make whatever use they want of their own talents. They can do as little as they can get away with – get to work right on time, leave right on time, and do only those tasks explicitly stated in their job description.

However, if they choose, they can, by their initiative, try to make themselves indispensable to the company. The one thing we must avoid is drawing up a mental bill of rights and then insisting that these rights be recognized and observed every minute of the day.

Working Effectively

We have become accustomed to working under pressure and we expend much more energy than we need to. Tension has become such a habit with people that much if not all of it is below the level of consciousness. Some even believe that tense and unrelaxed efforts result in more productivity. We associate tension with effort, and many of us feel that we're not working hard enough if we don't feel strained.

The truth, of course, if just the opposite. When we relax, we can do the same amount of work better and with less effort and we won't be worn out by the end of the day. First of all, work suffers when it is done under pressure. We're simply not thinking or performing at our best.

Some of our tension is caused by that feeling that we're always behind. We never seem to be able to "catch up" with our work. It's true that many jobs are very demanding, but part of the problem is that we don't understand that the very nature of work means that something is always happening. If we ever got "caught up" it would mean that we had come to a standstill.

In order for something to be accomplished, somebody has to roll up their sleeves and get to work. Great men do not set out to work because they are inspired – they become inspired because they are working.

When you are performing a work related task, be concerned about the project itself and not the outcome. Working at a steady pace with confidence will get the job done. Deliberately easing off on manifestations of tension, lowering your voice, and not worrying about success or failure in a particular project will produce a better result with you feeling less exhausted when the job is complete.

Accepting Criticism

Have you ever felt like walking out on your job? A lot of people feel that way from time to time and, unfortunately, some people do just that, only to regret it later. Quite a few people resist constructive criticism in varying degrees and, accordingly, are not able to profit from it.

I think it was Albert Einstein who said: "Don't tell me what I do right. I know that. What I need to know is what I do wrong." And as a result of his constant challenging of his own talents and findings, Einstein was able to open the eyes of the world.

Most employers will tell you that the ability and willingness to accept criticism is a key factor in determining whether a person should move upward in the company.

The Golden Rule Of Success

I'm sure most of us have heard somebody say: "Sure, I could do a better job if they paid me for it. But only a chump does something he isn't paid for." I've always wondered about people who have an attitude like that. Their remark about doing better if they're paid for it, sums up their mistake. That just isn't how the system works. You don't get a raise by promising better performance – you get it by demonstrating better performance.

You can't harvest success unless you plant the seed of success. And the seed of success is *service*. People who put service first find that success takes care of itself. Consider the people with whom you do business. The reason you deal with them instead of their competitors – even though you might have to pay a little more – is that you feel they offer you more and better quality service. How many of us have said to ourselves: "I don't mind the price as long as I get value."

Here is the simple but powerful rule that has helped a lot of people develop the put-service-first attitude: *Always give people more than they expect to get.* Each little extra something you do is a seed of success that will eventually pay you back with large dividends.

Persistence

What do you think is credited most often for success? Luck? An original idea? A rich uncle? These things work sometimes. But most successful men trace their success to one character trait – *persistence.* Often the successful person has no more talent that anyone else. What he does have is the ability to keep going no matter what happens.

The blend of success contains many things. A certain degree of talent or skill is needed, as is a willingness to work. But you can possess all those things necessary for success and still fail if you lack perseverance.

Without persistence the electric light bulb might not have come along when it did. Thomas Edison was ridiculed by the press all over the world for his repeated failures to perfect a fila-ment for the bulb. Well, while others ridiculed, Edison pressed on. And after about 3,000 failures, he found something that worked.

This ethic was expressed well by Samuel Johnson: "*Great works are performed not by strength but by perseverance*".

Effective Leadership

To be an effective leader, four qualities are essential.

- You must have self-control. In order to control others, you must first be in control of yourself.

- You must have controlled flexibility. You must be willing to stick by your decisions, but at the same time, you must be willing to change them if the situation changes. A person who is firm in his decisions shows courage. The person who will change decisions for good reasons shows fair-mindedness.

- You must be understanding. You can't shut yourself off from your subordinates. You must see to their problems, protect group norms, and give whatever help you can.

- You must be a planner. You have to anticipate problems and try to have solutions ready in advance.

If you can accomplish these things on a day to day basis, you may be able to develop a strong and committed work force.

Chapter 8

RELATIONSHIPS

QUALITY OF LIFE seems to be what most people seek. This entity can be found in different forms for each individual. For some it is money, for some, fame, and for others, securing a position in life that provides some personal gratification or emotional reward.

There is, however, one common thread that seems to unite us all in our quest. The most exquisite life quality is found in *relationships.* Whether the relationships are the bond between friends, the common goals sought by co-workers, or the most elusive, yet most rewarding of all, the romantic relationship; the knowledge that you may have found your *life partner*; the interaction between two people is second to none in making a life worthwhile.

The most beautiful relationships I have ever seen are those in which people accept each other for what they are, rather than analyzing everything they do. While sharing thoughts and feelings is a beautiful experience to be encouraged, it should not be "pushed" as a regular duty. I believe that a great many relationships are overanalyzed these days, and that is why, for many couples, being together is more torment than passion.

The fact is that you are two different people and you will never completely understand each other, nor should you. So why not work at accepting each other for what you are, and stop the hashing, re-hashing, analyzing and trying to "work on" the relationship. Let each other be unique, and as Kahlil Gibran said, "*Let there be spaces in your togetherness."*

Your relationships to other people are the single most important part of your life. When you experience a strong negative or positive emotion, it is almost always related to another person, be it a spouse, parent, child, or employer.

You know you need friends. But it isn't enough to surround yourself with a group of acquaintances who may or may not be there when a crisis occurs. You need people you can really count on. The strongest friendships must go deeper than having a good time, participating in social activities, or perhaps even the exchange of mutual confidences. They must encompass lasting beliefs and values and a demonstrated willingness to give as well as to receive.

One powerful aspect of strong social supports is the feeling of being loved, cared for, and valued. When something happens to threaten your self-esteem or make you feel unloved, the reassurance of loving friends appears to be a major factor in maintaining equilibrium. The most effective support you can give, researchers have found, comes simply from listening and encouraging the expressions of feelings without advice or judgment.

Stress

In the 1960's, Thomas H. Holmes and Richard H. Rahe of the University of Washington School of Medicine definitively established a correlation between stressful life events and disease. The researchers found that any change, whether for better or for worse, produced stress. Stress is the body's response to any demand for change, whether the change is pleasant or unpleasant.

The body's reaction to stress has been called the General Adaptation Syndrome (GAS). The first stage of the GAS, the *alarm reaction*, occurs whenever a real or perceived threat triggers an emergency discharge of adrenaline and sets off other physiological mechanisms the body requires to stay in control.

The muscles tense, the heart beats faster, the rate of respiration increases, the stomach may clench. We all, I'm sure, have experienced these feelings at one time or another.

Generally, the most acute signs of the stress reaction pass quickly and a normal level of functioning is restored when the threat subsides. But if it continues, the body enters the stage of *resistance* and efforts to adapt are intensified. The body is now weakened and open to illness. If there is still no relief, a third stage, *exhaustion*, follows due to fatigue and damage to the body.

Stress does not *cause* disease but, by exhausting the body's natural defenses against infection, it sets the stage for it. That is how your interpersonal relationships, like other stressors in your life, can make you more susceptible to illness. By improving your own relationships, you can lessen the likelihood that this will happen.

Despite the potential for stress in close, personal relationships, it's becoming increasingly clear that healthy, long lives, depend on strengthening our bonds with others. A full and rewarding social life can nourish the mind, the emotions, and the spirit, and good physical health depends as much on these aspects of ourselves as it does on a strong and well-functioning body.

It seems likely that when stress levels are low, social support may have relatively little effect on health but during periods of high stress the presence of a good social support system can significantly affect your physical well-being.

In other words, if things are going well in all areas of your life, you may not need much in the way of social support. But, if you lose your job or your spouse leaves you, close relationships with others can help you withstand the stress.

It's normal to feel depressed and to experience deep feelings of grief when you lose someone you love. But despair – which goes beyond depression into an attitude of hopelessness – has been found to correlate with the development of cancer.

According to Lawrence LeShan, Ph.D., the despairing person

feels hopeless about ever achieving any meaning or validity in life. They regard relationships as inevitably leading to disappointment and pain.

O. Carl Simonton, M.D., whose revolutionary and controversial approach to cancer treatment has attracted widespread attention, also believes that "cancer is often an indication of problems elsewhere in a person's life, problems aggravated and compounded by a series of stresses six to eighteen months prior to the onset of cancer."

While he acknowledges that external agents such as radiation, genetics, and diet may all play a role into the causes of cancer, Dr. Simonton feels that none of these factors explain fully why particular individuals, at particular points in their lives, develop cancer.

One clue is the fact that lymphocyte function, a critical measure of the body's immune system, is significantly depressed in those who have suffered severe stress. Chronic stress suppresses the immune system which is responsible for destroying abnormal cells, thus leaving the body more vulnerable to the growth of cancer.

While we cannot control everything that happens to us, we can consciously choose our reactions. By assuming the role of a victim we increase our body's vulnerability to disease.

No one argues that you can get cancer or hypertension just because you're feeling depressed, but emotions clearly contribute to the onset and course of the disease; it's dead wrong to call it folklore.

It is a well-researched fact that external events that do not actually touch our bodies can drastically affect our health because of the physiological responses evoked by our attitudes and emotions toward such events. Our brain produces its own morphine-like substances, such as endorphins, which not only kill pain but produce powerful, good feelings, even euphoria.

Swiss researcher Hugo Besedovsky found dramatic rises in the electrical activity in animal brains when the immune system goes into action; neuroscientist Karen Bulloch located the neurological communication pathways between the brain and the immune system; and J. Edwin Blalock discovered that immune cells produce the same chemical hormones previously thought to be only in the brain. What all of these findings tell us is that when an experience registers in the brain, it triggers electrical and chemical messages that may also travel to and affect the immune system, the body's first line of defense against infections.

Evidence tells us that feelings of hopelessness and helplessness can be a significant health risk, while joy, optimism, and a sense of commitment seem to be good for physical and emotional health. It is now clear that hostile, "Type A" people, who respond to life's tensions with aggression and anger, are more likely to experience higher cholesterol, triglyceride, and catecholamine levels – all known to be triggered by prolonged stress – which lead to increased risk of coronary problems. In fact, the greater the hostility, the greater the amount of cholesterol clogging the arteries, the worse the angina symptoms, and the more frequent and severe the heart attacks.

Out of the field of mind-body experiences comes the discovery that not only our individual emotions but our emotional ties to each other affect our physical well-being. Studies have revealed a dramatic decrease in health problems and death rates for people who are socially involved, compared with those who are isolated.

Although research has established the links between our minds and our bodies, and the effect our emotional ties with others have on our health, few people have adopted the kinds of behaviors that use this knowledge wisely and get the healthful break from tension that we need. Most of us live with a great deal of stress, showing up as tension, tight muscles, back pain and diverse other symptoms. We need a reduction in stress that involves our daily way of looking at and interacting with others.

Just as hostility and other negative attitudes can lead to ill health, there are also emotions that can enhance health and lower the risk of disease by counteracting the effects of stress and creating positive bodily reactions. Among these good-health emotions are trust, feelings of self-worth, self-control, self-determination, a sense of challenge and commitment, optimism, and joyfulness.

Exercise and good nutrition, for all their worth in keeping us healthy, are not enough. We must be able to bring our awareness to the positive health potential of helping others.

Being Yourself

It's impossible to overstate – for your peace of mind, your health, and your self-respect - the importance of loving your relationship and being able to be *Yourself.* No one said it better that William Shakespeare: *"To thine own self be true."*

Relationships can only be real if you are real and accept and recognize your own feelings. In the course of learning to accept your own feelings and attitudes, you grow in your capacity to understand and accept the feelings and attitudes of others.

Before you can become a loving person, you must love yourself, and this means becoming your own unique self. It's an exciting process, but seldom an easy one because being yourself does not mean staying the same. All of life is a process of growth and change, of trusting your own experience and intuitive feelings to lead you in the direction that will allow you most fully to become yourself. As a result, your relationships will become deeper and more meaningful. Because when you give yourself up for someone else, or to live up to some else's standards your resentment will express itself psychologically and somatically.

Balancing Your Life

Many people in our society spend their day getting up, going to work, grabbing a newspaper when they get home, eating dinner, and sitting in front of the television until bedtime. Chances are, people who follow this routine over a long period of time find it difficult to deal with tension. They are in a rut and they haven't set time aside for their minds to unwind.

If you think you might be in a similar rut, it might be time to find some pastime or hobby. You would be surprised at the number of things going on that would serve well to relieve your tensions. Getting involved in an interest outside of your daily routine is relaxing and mentally stimulating, both of which are vital for effective living.

Touching

Because physical contact is so important in establishing and maintaining emotional bonding, it's unfortunate that we so often neglect this source of comfort and closeness within a relationship.

Touching can make us feel warm, secure, and loved. And it is highly probable that physical contact also provides important health benefits.

I say "highly probable" because it is difficult to sort out the contribution of physical contact from other beneficial aspects of close personal relationships. Common sense tells us that it is effective in relieving anxiety and providing emotional comfort. We all know what a hug or a touch of the hand can do when we're feeling down.

The tenderness of a touch can show affection but touching by itself is not necessarily a reflection of feeling. Touch can be for physical reasons alone – to satisfy physical needs – as opposed to coming from the heart.

There is a difference between a touch that becomes increasingly heartfelt over a period of time between two people and the satisfaction of animal needs which we certainly all have. But those basic needs are meaningless without affection.

How Good Is Your Relationship?

Sometimes the indication that something is wrong in your life or in an important relationship isn't a symptom or an illness, or even an emotional state such as depression or anxiety. Perhaps it is just a behavior pattern that you (or someone else) recognizes as unhealthy or undesirable.

"That's just the way I am," a partner may say in describing a problem behavior; "And there's nothing I can do about it." But there is. If you **want** to change a behavior pattern, you can do so. Take, for example, temper outbursts. Too often the excuse is, "You know I've got a bad temper; I just can't control it."

But most of these bad tempered people never lose control at work or with their friends, which proves that they can remain in charge of their behavior when they deem it necessary. Here are some signs that you have a behavioral problem.

- You often regret losing your temper.

- You use sleep as an escape.

- People you live with often complain about your messiness.

- You procrastinate a lot.

- You do more than your share of complaining.

If these symptoms sound familiar, you need to work on correcting your behavior because the cost of inconsiderate behavior towards people close to you is usually losing them.

A good, compatible relationship is essential to physical and emotional health. The answers to the following statements should be yes in any healthy relationship. If you must say in total honesty that they don't apply to you, then you have a problem and need to decide how much of your life you are willing to waste. Remember, if you aren't honest about your answers to these questions, you are only fooling yourself.

- On the whole, would you rate your relationship as very happy?

- Have you ever seriously considered ending the relationship?

- If you had to do it over, would you enter the same relationship again?

- Can you rely on your partner to keep his (her) promises?

- Are you in agreement on most really important issues and values?

- Does your partner respect your beliefs and wishes, even when you differ?

- Can you trust your partner not to make an important decision without consulting you?

- Is your sexual relationship satisfying to both of you?

- Can you count on your partner to be sexually faithful?

- Is your partner definitely concerned with your happiness?

- Do you enjoy spending leisure time together?

- Do you laugh a lot together?

- Would your partner sense it if something were bothering you, even if you didn't bring it up?

- Can you trust you partner not to repeat anything you confide?

- Does your partner listen attentively when you have something to say?

- Does your partner ever put you down?

- Is your partner interested in your daily activities?

- Does your partner treat your family and friends with

respect?

- If you wrote a book, would your partner would be eager to read it?

- Does your partner respect you as a separate individual?

- Is your partner proud of you?

Now read the following statements and see if they apply to your current relationship. If they are true, then ask yourself why you are still with a partner who makes you feel this way.

- My partner abuses me verbally with shouting, insults, or name-calling.

- We have loud, upsetting arguments.

- I have had to leave the house to end an argument.

- My partner is sarcastic toward me.

- I feel resentful toward my partner.

- When my partner comes home, I feel myself tensing up.

- I look forward to my partner's absence from home.

- There are things about my partner that really disgust me.

- My partner's treatment of me is damaging to my self-esteem.

- My partner makes me cry.

Expressing Yourself

Learning to express yourself about your own feelings and needs is absolutely essential to a good relationship. That doesn't mean to ignore the feelings of other people; simply to give your own feelings equal consideration.

Within a personal relationship, important feelings must be expressed. A small annoyance about some episode that may never occur again is best ignored. After all, you shouldn't get in the habit of complaining about everything.

When To Let Go

Sometimes you can't see the forest for the trees. You are so absorbed in trying to solve relationship problems that you don't realize you are dealing with a deeply disturbed person whom you cannot possibly change and with whom you really don't wish to continue living. The world is full of extremely troubled people with excellent defenses and ways to cover up their disturbances.

In these cases, the solution is not learning to deal with the problems. The relationship is just a mistake. You need to become astute enough psychologically to distinguish problems you can work on from those you can't.

Chapter 9

BELIEVING IN LOVE

ALTHOUGH THERE ARE many definitions and styles of love, from the perspective of the real inner self and its development, love is the capacity to acknowledge the other person in a warm, affectionate way, with no strings attached and to enjoy the sexual passion that energizes the relationship in such a way that the welfare of the partner, in every sense of that term, becomes as important as one's own welfare. To love is to like, to approve of, and to support another's true inner self and encourage them to activate, express, and nurture themselves.

The initial attraction which sets one person apart from the many people we meet in our day to day life is usually an intense hormonal attraction. There is no logical explanation as to why one certain individual appeals to us in such a special way. Physical appearance is probably one factor although this is a subjective opinion. If the opportunity to spend time which the object of our attraction presents itself, we will find ourselves advancing to the next stage of a potential relationship.

Genuine intimacy seems to develop in the early overtures two people make to each other. As we sift through and test the responses we get in these first encounters, we look to see how the other person appreciates or fails to appreciate us. When the feedback is positive, affectionate and sexual feelings usually intensify along with a growing willingness on the part of the two people to become more intimately involved with each other on all levels.

Inevitably, sex will become a part of the relationship and can be a powerful emotional experience that brings people even closer together. However, when sex is the key component in a relationship, people tend to be self-serving, using the other person to gratify their own needs. In fact, a relationship that turns sexual early on, or even begins as a sexual relationship, has the power to blind the couple to the realities about each other and how they function together so that the sorting out of positive and negative factors that are necessary to make an honest commitment based on knowledge and understanding never takes place.

One of the most gratifying aspects of being in touch with your emotions is the ability to experience the feelings brought on by your relationships with others. The most powerful of these feelings is the intimacy that can result from an attraction to another human being.

The adult human is capable of forming a powerful and lasting bond of attachment for a member of the opposite sex that is much more than a mere "partnership". To say that marriage, for example, is a partnership, as is so often stated, is to insult it, and to completely misunderstand the true nature of a bond of love. In a partnership, one merely exchanges favors; the partner does not give for the sake of giving. There is no 'give and take' in the true loving, only giving. The fact that it is 'two way giving' obscures this, but the 'two way receiving' that inevitably results from it is not a condition of the giving, as it is in a 'partnership'; it is simply a pleasing benefit of it.

For the cautious, calculating adult, the entry into such a relationship is a hazardous affair. The resistance to 'letting go' and trusting is enormous. It breaks all of the rules of bargaining and dealing that is used in all other adult relationships. Without some help from the lower centers of the brain, the higher centers would never permit it.

For some, the natural process of 'falling in love' is suppressed, and if a couple does enter into a state of marriage or it's equivalent, the couple does so as if it were a business transaction: "you look after the house and the children, I will earn the money". The mated pair are held together, not by bonds of attachment, but by the external pressures of social convention. This means that the couple's natural potential for falling in love still lies waiting inside their brains and can leap into action without warning at any time, to create a true bond somewhere outside their official one.

For the lucky people, this sequence does not take place. The process of falling in love is a gradual one, although it does not always appear to be. 'Love at first sight' is a popular concept. It is, however, usually a retrospective judgment. What occurs is not 'total trust at first sight', but 'powerful attraction at first sight'. The progress from first attraction to final trust is nearly always a long and complex sequence of gradually increasing intimacies.

Most of these intimacies exclude all aspects of practicality and are simply the result of growing closeness and a constant desire to do everything in your power to make your partner happy and show them that, to you, there is no one in the world more wonderful and special than they are.

Unfortunately, when the special person; the 'one who was meant for them' comes into the picture, often times they are already immersed in a relationship based primarily on practical and comfort issues. These relationships have no special qualities to them, no passion, and usually no love in the true definition of the feeling.

What results then is a forced decision as to whether they should stay in the present relationship or follow their emotions and fulfill the opportunity to spend the rest of their days with the wonderful feeling that they are with the partner they were meant to be with; the one whose simple words or looks can make their life take on a whole new meaning.

It is, however, not wise to respond to your feelings with no thought to the practical aspects of your brain. Certain qualities of a relationship must be present to ensure a reasonable chance for longevity. There must be common interests between you and your true love. Pay no heed to ancient adage, 'opposites attract.' They may very well attract each other but offer almost no chance for a happy and enduring life together. There must first, last, and foremost, be a mutual respect for each other. Common sense must play a part when making decisions which will have a drastic effect on the happiness sought from a life-long relationship.

Love is viewed as a fundamental part of nature. The beauty of springtime; a walk along the river path; sitting in a quiet place somewhere; love as we knew it long ago was perhaps more meaningful because it seemed to be identified with the beauty of the surroundings. Love was identified with the natural world. We associated love and nature; nature sort of conditioned our feelings and emotions. Love was just an outgrowth of everything else that was beautiful.

Sometimes, making a difference is part of what belief in love is all about. Sometimes you can solve problems; sometimes they can't be solved, but you figure out ways to live with the difficulties. You don't let problems undermine your sense of good in relationships. Love is loyalty. Love is teamwork. Love respects the dignity of the individual.

There is a component of love that is not at the verbal level. It is beyond the scope of words. Some parts of the human experience are so intense or so delicate that we are unable to express them accurately within the mode of language.

The elements of love that are beyond language are similar to some physical phenomena that are beyond comprehension to the average person. Distances in the solar system, for example, are measured in light-years. But how many people understand the distances so vast they must be measured in astronomical units equal to 6,000,000,000,000 miles? It is, in a sense, something beyond comprehension. The nonverbal aspects of love define the human experience of emotion and relationships. Visual arts; painting, sculpture, and architecture provide the mirror.

People are born with different temperaments and different natural abilities. Some people are naturally athletic, a talent that is evident from the time they are young. Others may be naturally musical, artistic or mathematical. Often when someone has a strong natural ability, it is accompanied by a belief in how important it is. Some people have a natural ability to love. As they travel through life, their belief in love continues.

Such people should be classified as "true positives." That is, the way they appear to be on the outside (loving) is the way they are on the inside (loving). They choose to live their lives that way. While they are not perfect, there is something different about them in terms of human relationships. The difference shows up most in the influence they have on others. The effect they have on others is nurturing.

For years, social scientists have attempted to explain why people are the way they are. A controversy emerged over nature versus nurture in determining human personality and behavior, which resulted in three different theoretical positions.

The first one focuses on nature and suggests that people are born with a temperament based on the influence of genetics. The second one emphasizes environment: people develop as a result of what they learn from their relationships with their parents, culture, and so on. The third position involves a combination of both nature and nurture.

Explaining human nature is very difficult, partly because research on humans is so complex. In social science, unlike physical science, we are limited in how we can explain the wide variation in human behavior.

To maintain a belief in love, a person needs to learn to deal with the potential pain of being emotionally vulnerable without surrounding their heart with armor. Emotional risk-taking can take the form of sharing feelings, telling the other person about their importance to you, revealing hidden worries and fears. The feeling of being loved intimately and having a trusted confidant can contribute to our self-esteem and our sense of control over our fears, even during high-stress situations.

No one discovers or invents love. Love discovers us. It demands that a person relax their internal defenses to believe in a power or goodness beyond themselves.

The point of this is not that some people should not be together and should avoid each other, but that many of the problems that couples have, whether well matched or not, are due to ignorance of how to live with each other's temperaments.

It is sometimes difficult to believe in love. To do so requires much courage because the experience of love can bring much devastating pain. To maintain a belief in love, a person needs to learn to deal with the potential pain of being emotionally vulnerable.

Love is the chaos theory of human relationships. Daily life seems fairly normal and organized around routine and principles, and then along comes love and changes everything. Sometimes it is just the unknown, accompanied by a general state of confusion.

Many times love doesn't work because some people have an expectation of "safe love." They expect that love can be obtained without taking much risk: without revealing one's self, sharing one's feelings, accepting one's vulnerability. And all of these things are very difficult to do. The very nature of love involves a risk of self-revelation.

Someone who understands love recognizes that a relationship with another person is affected by their relationship with themselves. As a result, they try to continue to grow in the area of self-awareness. 'The more I understand myself, the better I am able do deal with problems that may occur in my life'. This reminds me of a quotation by Henry David Thoreau: "If a man does not keep pace with his companions, perhaps it is because he hears a different drummer. Let him step to the music that he hears, however measured or far away."

Chapter 10

LIVE NOW

Why We Need Others

LONELINESS IS A burden to many people, but we cease to be alone the moment we start to care about others. One of the strangest things about the age we live in is the fact that so many people seem determined to be lonely. Maybe it has something to do with how busy we all are, but whatever the cause, there seem to be thousands of people building walls around their lives and around their hearts.

Almost every day we hear somebody say, "It's none of my business," or "Leave me out of it," or "I don't want to get involved." These people seem almost terrified of the complications that may come from getting mixed up in someone else's life. Or perhaps they dread the possibility of being rejected if they hold out a hand to another human being.

No one likes to feel that they are standing alone on the dark edge of the world. And no one can feel alone if their life touches the life of someone else. When we look around us, we can see that the fullest and richest moments come when people are involved with one another. Joy multiplies when you share it; grief, when you share it, becomes smaller. We are truly alive only to the extent that we are involved with other people.

William Wordsworth said: "*The best portions of a good life are little, nameless, unremembered acts of kindness and love."* Small acts of kindness may not appear to have much value, but they are important psychologically: "Let people recognize that every man who is kind, helpful, decent, psychologically democratic, affectionate and warm is a psycho-therapeutic force."

By demonstrating simple kindnesses to people we deal with we are acting as a little psychological tonic for them. And vice versa. A gruff approach to people serves in a small way to hurt them psychologically. Kindness begets kindness. By acting with kindness and consideration, we are likely to be treated in a similar manner by those we deal with. And, of course, we would personally benefit from this small psychological boost.

I think one of the reasons we fail to say the kind word or show any tenderness toward our fellow human beings is that this is an age where we're intent on appearing sophisticated. We feel that any sentiment will be either rebuffed or misunderstood. We feel humiliation. We consider it so important to act tough and dignified that we repress our real feelings and hide behind a mask of indifference and flippancy.

I have a habit of writing down meaningful passages I come across in my reading. One of my favorites is the German poet Goethe: *"Correction does much, but encouragement does more. Encouragement after censure is as the sun after a shower."* Most of us tend to forget just how important encouragement is, probably because so much of life is concerned with criticizing and correcting and finding fault with others.

The word *encourage* comes from the French word for heart. Thus to encourage someone is to put strength into his heart. This can have great meaning in our daily lives. There are literally thousands of ways to give courage to our fellow man every day in the office, in the market-place, and in the street. A gesture, a smile, a wave of the hand, a kind word are all small but meaningful signs of encouragement.

When we pause to consider how much we, individually, need encouragement, then it becomes easier to realize how important it is for each of us, individually, to give heart to others.

Today is that time when the past and the future meet. It is the only time in which we can live. It is essential to make the most of it.

Today – right now – this minute is our life. If we think we're delaying our real living until some future time when all our problems will be solved, then we're kidding ourselves. There's an old saying: *"The wise man knows that today is living, while the fool is always getting prepared to live."*

Today is the day to tell your wife that you appreciate her as a person, and that you know how hard she's been working.

Today is the day to tell your husband that you realize the pressure he's under in this modern world, and you know he's beating his brains out.

Today is the day to tell your child that you know how hard he's studying and you're proud of him.

Today is the day to look around you and decide to start living.

Emerson said: "Every hour has its morning, noon, and night." And we can take the morning of the very next hour and do with that hour something we can remember for the rest of our lives. There is only one effective way to get ready for tomorrow, and that is by doing something today.

Many years ago, the philosopher, Epicurus, said: *"The fool does not so much live as always get ready to live. And then one day it is too late."* Most of us fall into this trap at one time or another. And some of us are doing it right now. We think we can get things in perfect order and then sit down to the banquet of perfection that we have created and enjoy life. But this can never happen. We no sooner get one problem solved than things come unstuck someplace else, and then we have to postpone living all over again. We no sooner get so we can make ends meet than they move the ends.

If you're waiting for some magic day when you have every problem nailed down, then you'll be waiting for your whole life. Life will never be simple or perfect. There is only one time that any of us ever have to do anything, and that time is now. If you decide to wait one more week, one more day, or one more minute, you are misleading and cheating yourself.

- Now is the only time to empty your mind of all its resentments and start living.

- Now is the only time to give the world and everyone in it – including yourself – a blanket forgiveness and start to live new and fresh.

- Now is the time for all of us to become the person we want to be but have put off until later.

People and living things are all that matter. Without life around you to share, you have no possibility for joy. If you took away life, there would be nothing in the world to have or give meaning. Life is all that counts.

Chapter 11

Intellect, Intelligence And Emotion

WEBSTER'S DICTIONARY DEFINES intellect as intelligence and intelligence as the ability or capacity to learn and understand. These definitions do not satisfy some of the questions I have regarding the co-relation between the two. Explain to me why identical twins who share the same appearance and physical traits and were raised in exactly the same way are two totally different people deep inside, or why a man with Albert Einstein's mental capacity could not remember his own street address.

After much research and comparative analysis, I think that intellect must be described as the soul or essence of a person. That indefinable quality that was not created through heredity or environment. By way of comparison, intelligence must be the capacity to learn and intellect is the will to use this ability and put the knowledge to the best possible use. By way of analogy, I define intellect as the tradesman and intelligence as the quality of tools used in the trade.

Intellect, I think, is the absolute differential between individuals. We may all have similar, but not identical, feelings and reactions to events or actions. Some of us are more affected or less affected by circumstances and situations we are privy to or involved in. The purest form of intelligence without intellect or emotion would be an autistic savant such as the one portrayed by Dustin Hoffman in the movie, "Rainman". His brain functioned at an extremely high level, compiling and computing factual information with no balance of use or application. He could multiply 23,596 times 28,422 instantly but couldn't tell you what two plus two was. Although the character was fictional, the persona was real. His emotional outbursts were not a result of emotions at all; merely a reaction to a change in external stimuli.

Now enter the wild card; Emotion; which, in my opinion does not alter a person's intelligence level, but definitely has an effect on their intellect when faced with an emotional situation. A person's intelligence dictates to them the logical thing to do to achieve the best possible result. However, their emotions sometimes cause them to act in an inappropriate way even though they know the emotional reaction will likely not have the same result as a logical reaction would. Without the intellect, which can be affected by emotion, people would react as would robots. All actions and events would lead to the same reaction. Intellect causes people to prioritize their retained knowledge so that information and facts used on a regular basis are easily recalled and unused knowledge, although still present in the memory, does not surface to the conscious level of the brain as readily. Significant events in a person's life seem always to be there in the forefront of the memory, probably because we think often of these events, albeit, subconsciously.

Emotional Intelligence

Fundamental ethical stances in life stem from underlying emotions. For one, impulse is the medium of emotion; the seed of all impulse is a feeling bursting to express itself in action. Those who are at the mercy of impulse; who lack self-control, suffer a moral deficiency. The ability to control impulse is the basis of will and character. By the same token, the root of altruism lies in empathy, the ability to read emotions in others. When lacking a sense of another 's need or despair, there is no caring. And if there are any two moral stances that are necessary to survive emotionally in today's world, they are self-restraint and compassion.

The most common and easily recognizable reaction to situational distress is anger. The lack of ability to deal with disagreeable occurrences or responses from another person will manifest itself in the form of anger varying in level from challenging verbal assaults to physical violence. The presence of this anger disables the brain's ability to deal sensibly with the situation and it's purpose is usually to create enough fear in the other parties involved so that attention is diverted away from the real issue at hand.

Emotional intelligence is the ability to rein in emotional impulse; to read another's innermost feelings; to handle relationships smoothly; or as Aristotle put it, *"The rare skill to be angry with the right person, to the right degree, at the right time, for the right purpose, and in the right way."* For many, the lack of emotional awareness is more than just a "character deficiency". It may be the result of a poor connection between the Limbic area of the brain and the Necrotic. The only feeling these people are able to express without thoughtful analysis is anger. There is no instinctive reaction to things of beauty, no joy in the pleasure of simple things, and no capability to have deep feelings for another human being.

The medical term for this deficiency is "Alexithymia". Those who are classified as Alexithymics are utterly lacking in the fundamental skill of emotional intelligence, self-awareness, the ability to express what they are feeling simply because they aren't sure what the feeling is. The frustration in this usually manifests itself as anger because the act of being angry will usually discourage questions for which they have no answer. Alexithymics lack empathy as well as insight. Confused about their own feelings, they are equally bewildered when other people express their feelings to them. Their lack of empathy renders them unable to feel the pain of others. In the most severe cases of Alexithymia, sociological tendencies emerge. These symptoms are most prevalent in molesters, rapists and sociopaths. The inability to feel their victim's pain allows them to tell themselves lies that encourage their crime. For rapists, the lies include "Women really want to be raped" or "If she resists, she's just playing hard to get".

The blotting out of empathy as these people inflict damage on their victims is almost always part of an emotional cycle that precipitates their cruel acts. The psychopath (more recently called the sociopath as a psychiatric diagnosis) is notorious for being both charming and completely without remorse for even the most cruel and heartless acts. Psychopathy: the incapacity to feel empathy or compassion of any sort, or the least twinge of conscience, is one of the more perplexing of emotional defects. The heart of the psychopath's coldness seems to lie in an inability to make anything more than the shallowest of emotional connections. Psychopaths are also glib liars, willing to say anything to get what they want, and they manipulate their victims' emotions with the same cynicism.

One of the more ominous ways the absence of empathy displays itself is in a study of wife batterers. Research revealed a physiological anomaly among many of the most violent husbands, who regularly beat up their wives or threatened them with physical harm. They did so in a cold calculating state rather than while being carried away by the heat of fury. As their anger mounted, the anomaly emerged: their heart rate dropped, instead of climbing, as is normally the case with mounting anger. This means they are growing physiologically calmer, even as they become more belligerent and abusive and their violence appeared to be a calculated act of terrorism, a method of controlling their wives by instilling fear.

Not all people are able to bond emotionally, although the number who fall statistically within this category is relatively small. In the extreme sense, people in this group have psychological disorders that interfere with maintaining relationships. Sociopaths and serial killers, for example, view people as objects to be exploited, not people to be related to. They are able to act out cruelty toward others because a necessary degree of emotionality is missing within them. They have difficulty relating to others. While they may pretend they understand and possess feelings, to a large degree, they don't. Most emotion is outside their range of conscious experience.

Some people are more naturally attuned to the emotional mind's special appreciation for the wonders of intangibles such as appreciation of poetry, song, and stories, all of which are cast in the language of the heart. So too, are dreams and myths, in which loose associations determine the flow of narrative, abiding by the logic of the emotional mind. Those who have a natural attunement to their own heart's voice - the language of emotion - are sure to be more adept at articulating its messages; whether as a novelist, songwriter, poet, or psychotherapist. Self-awareness is fundamental to psychological insight. Simply stated, you must be able to understand yourself before you can understand others.

Good people seem to stand out, perhaps more so because of the stressful times we live in today. The pressure and uncertainty make it hard: people are all struggling to achieve something, but once they get it they wonder what they've been striving for. In the meantime, they have missed out on some of the simple pleasures of life. It's important to smell the flowers along the way.

People who have found an appropriate balance between intelligence and emotion have a much greater chance of success in life than those with only a highly developed intelligence level. The emotional factors in decision making, problem solving, and inter-reactions with other people on all levels, make an individual more compatible with day-to-day life.

Social Competence

A key to social competence is how well or how poorly people express their own feelings. Emotions are contagious. Most emotional contagion is extremely subtle, part of a tacit exchange that happens in every encounter.

We transmit and catch moods from each other in what amounts to a subterranean level of the psyche in which some encounters are toxic, and some nourishing. This emotional exchange is typically at a subtle, almost imperceptible level; the way a salesperson says thank you can leave us feeling ignored, resented, or genuinely welcomed and appreciated. We catch feelings from each other as though they were some kind of social virus.

People who are poor at receiving and sending emotions are prone to problems in their relationships, since others often feel uncomfortable with them, even if they can't articulate just why this is so. Those who are adept in social intelligence can connect with people quite smoothly, be astute in reading reactions and feelings, lead and organize, and handle disputes that are bound to flare up in any human activity. They are the natural leaders, the kind of people others like to be with because they are emotionally nourishing.

Chapter 12

HIGHLY SENSITIVE PEOPLE

What Are Highly Sensitive People?

FOR THOSE OF you who are new to the idea, HSP's are the 15 to 20 percent of the human population born with a nervous system genetically designed to be more sensitive to subtleties, more prone to deep reflection, and therefore more easily overwhelmed by events that may seem commonplace to most people.

Their high sensitivity is an inherited tendency to process what comes to them through their senses in a very deep, subtle manner. It's not that their eyes and ears are better, but that they sort what comes in more carefully. They like to inspect, reflect, and ponder.

They also get more pleasure from the arts and from their own inner life.

The bad news is that if they are going to pick up on all the subtleties around them, they are also going to be overwhelmed by the high levels of persistent, complex stimulation. They are easily stressed in today's world.

They are also more sensitive to criticism; they process all input deeply, including information about their shortcomings. They are more easily made depressed or anxious due to traumas, processing those more deeply too. As a consequence, they may feel less hope and greater insecurity than those who do not reflect on experiences as thoroughly.

Sensitivity is perhaps the most basic of inherited traits, its presence particularly affects relationships. High sensitivity is a new name for the most widely researched inherited personality difference (known in the past as introversion-extroversion, shyness-boldness, etc.), in humans. Research highlights differences in the basic wiring of the nervous system.

The Negative Side

Highly sensitive people need to turn off some of their sensitivity to the needs of others. When they try to help everyone whom they sense needs it, they are bound to be affected by **overarousal**. This leads to insomnia and anxiety due to high levels of the stress hormone, cortisol, which leads to low levels of the neurotransmitter, serotonin, and then they get anxious, depressed and irritable. There goes the loving kindness, anyway, so they should choose the people who really need them.

Highly sensitive people have a strong tendency to put others first to such a degree that the wants and needs of others are more important than their own. They would rather be unhappy than see someone else in an intolerable situation. They feel pain at the plight of others and would do anything to ease the pain of the helpless and needy of the world.

One of the major problems with being a Highly Sensitive Person is **Gender Bias**. Males and females are cast in pre-conceived roles and this trend, which has predominated opinions for dozens of years is very difficult to bypass.

"He's a real man"- somehow you have to prove that this is you. That's the burden of men in today's culture, and much of this need to prove originates in boyhood, when sexism most narrowly defines the ideal male's behavior and thinking. A "real man" should be tough and cool; that is, to have no deep thoughts that don't conform to the opinion of the "cool" crowd. He should be spontaneous, recklessly impulsive, and not reflective. He should be fiercely competitive and outgoing without needing people or showing any vulnerability. He never cries and rarely shows any emotion, especially not fear, shame, or remorse. In short, he is not highly sensitive. And by that logic, a highly sensitive man is not a "real man."

"Real Men" are expected to have overly rigid boundaries-to pay little attention to other's needs, their emotional needs especially. At the same time, men are expected to meet the needs of women in particular-especially their need to be protected. It's that impossible contradiction again. No matter how overwhelmed a man has become, he must perform, especially if it is a woman's emotional needs he is attending to. He is overworked. His conscientiousness is taken advantage of. He is constantly saying yes and resenting it later.

We all need to express our feelings and find solutions to problems, including these gender-related problems.

A large part of the tradition is that the "man rules the roost." There is strong evidence that such marriages are less satisfying to both partners and are more likely to end in divorce. Another part of "male supremacy" in a relationship is that the man ignores any requests from a woman partner that he change. It brings about the "withdrawl" concept. Withdrawing occurs when one partner tries to speak honestly or intimately, including expressing a demand for change, and the other refuses to talk, turns away physically, or turns off emotionally. The truth is when women demand and men withdraw, the relationships are highly troubled, polarized, and likely to end.

A man is also a victim of "Love Shyness"; a term coined by sociologist Brian Gilmartin, who has discovered that there is a small but troubled group of heterosexual men who have become too shy to initiate a romantic sexual relationship, although they desperately want to. If you are "love shy," you simply expect to be rejected romantically, mainly because of your sensitivity.

Much of this stems from early childhood. All sensitive men without parental support and self-confidence in adulthood tend to be overly cautious, turning down opportunities out of excessive fear. They often seek shelter in the first career they stumble into, or in a hasty marriage. Once inside their safe places, they tend to stay put longer, even if the situation is not satisfying.

Sensitive People Are Important To Relationships

The reason sensitive people are valuable in relationships is fairly obvious - for example, they are conscientious, intuitive, aware of others' moods, and eager to think deeply about what is going on. Sensitive people process more information before acting, checking things out carefully and taking fewer impulsive risks.

Sensitive people notice subtleties, enjoying the good ones and changing the annoying ones, so that life together is better. They also prevent problems by noticing warning signs. They see the things that need to be fixed and try to correct them before they are completely broken.

Sensitive people are likely to want long-term relationships – they dislike change, rejecting or being rejected and they are aware that endings are inevitably painful, but are prepared to experience and encourage the personal growth required to maintain a good relationship.

The great thing about them is that they get true, pure pleasure from the joy of others. Yes, they will sacrifice their own wants to accede to the desires of others but this makes them happy. To see someone they care about being totally satisfied with a situation makes their life complete. This is truly a person who loves to give, as much for his or her own pleasure as for the gratification of the receiver.

Choosing Well (Or Who Not To Fall In Love With)

None of what follows is reason enough to have or avoid a relationship with someone, but they are good guidelines. Sensitive people have a great deal of sympathy for everyone, gratitude for any kindness shown, and sometimes, a readiness to "settle for what they can get," being unsure that they will ever find anyone who could love such an "overly sensitive" person. Meanwhile, someone who could really appreciate them is waiting just around the corner.

- Try to find someone with an attachment style much like your own.

- A friendship with a person of a different culture can be terrific, but an exclusive, lifelong relationship will cause disagreements and strains you have never imagined.

- Pay attention to the person's work history. Dozens of stories about being fired or having to quit because of feeling victimized does not suggest good work relationships. Romantic partnerships involve working together, too.

- Beware of those who only talk about themselves and show little empathy for you.

- Beware of people obsessed with their own physical appearance.

- Avoid someone who has violently angry outbursts, even if they are rare. They probably will become much less rare.

Chapter 13

I Feel S.A.D. (Social Anxiety Disorder)

WE'VE ALL HAD experience with *shyness* or felt the symptoms ourselves to some degree. What you may not know is that in the extreme, there are some twenty million people in North America who suffer from the most radical form of it. It's known as *Social Anxiety Disorder*, also called *Social Phobia*. It's the most common anxiety disorder and the third most common psychiatric disorder overall. People suffering from it also run a greater risk for other problems such as depression, substance abuse or even suicide.

Most people have had butterflies in their stomach before giving a speech or have felt a little nervous on a first date but these natural reactions don't come close to the extreme fear and anxiety experienced by people with S.A.D. or social phobia. Thus, some social anxiety is normal and beneficial. After all, people who never care about others' opinions are often not very pleasant to be around.

But the experience of apprehension or worry that arises from the possibility that we will be evaluated or judged in some manner by others causes significant and persistent fear of social situations in which embarrassment or rejection may occur in S.A.D. sufferers. They will actually suffer physical reactions even though their fears may be mostly imagined or greatly exaggerated.

Someone may fear just one or two social encounters – public speaking being a common example. The problem is then referred to as *specific* or *discrete* social phobia. In contrast, *generalized* social anxiety exists when a person is afraid and avoids most social situations.

Symptoms can vary with the individual but they generally fall into three categories: the cognitive or mental symptoms (what you think); the physical reactions (how your body feels); and the behavioral avoidance (what you do).

People with this phobia are plagued with negative thoughts and doubts about themselves such as:

- Do I look okay?

- Am I dressed appropriately?

- Will I know what to talk bout?

- Will I sound stupid or boring?

- Will other people like me?

- Will people notice I'm nervous?

Some of the physical symptoms are shortness of breath, tightness or pain in the chest, racing heart, tingling sensations or numbness, nausea, diarrhea, dizziness, shaking, and sweating.

Regardless of which particular physical symptoms someone experiences, anxiety is never pleasant. Having one's body in a state of constant alert takes its toll and can lead to chronic fatigue, muscle tension, and sleep disturbances. These people make decisions in life based upon what they're comfortable with rather that what they might really want to do.

What Causes S.A.D.?

The predominant question is "What caused this?" It's a natural reaction because knowing the reason for a problem provides a sense of control and predictability.

There are two major factors that cause this disorder – biology (or genetics) and environment. Your biological makeup and life experiences combine and interact in such a way that it's difficult to separate them.

One of the ways to test for the genetic basis of a disorder is through the study of twins. Monozygotic, or identical twins share the exact same genetic makeup. Dizygotic, or fraternal twins are no more genetically similar than are any other siblings. If a certain condition occurs more commonly in identical twins as compared to fraternal twins, this indicates a genetic component.

Temperament

Temperament is one's inborn tendency to respond to the environment in a characteristic manner. The aspect of temperament that relates to how someone acts is called "behavioral inhibition." This refers to the tendency to be cautious in unfamiliar circumstances. When you're confronted with a situation, you stop and check to see if everything seems to be as you expect. If something seems out of place or unusual, you tend to move away.

Although it seems to indicate that temperament can make a person more prone to social anxiety, it is not, in itself, enough to cause the problem. You must keep in mind that behavioral inhibition isn't all bad. We need some people in the world who don't impulsively jump into every situation without forethought.

If, however, you are plagued consistently with the following or similar beliefs, you may be a victim of social phobia.

- My worth depends upon what others think of me.

- My worth depends upon my accomplishments.

- Anxiety and fear are signs of weakness.

- I cannot function when I am anxious.

- I cannot tolerate criticism or rejection.

- Everyone must like me or I cannot stand it.

You should, instead, consider the following things as more important than your fears:

- It's important to me to be a loving member of my family and nurture and take care of them as best I can.

- It's important to me to live a moral life, to be kind to others, and to help those in need.

- It's important to me to use my strengths and talents as best I can, not only in my work but in everything I do.

Many people with S.A.D. recall a specific traumatic event associated with the onset of their problems. This could be an instance of bullying, parenting style, an embarrassing relationship situation or any other humiliating scenario during a vulnerable period in one's earlier life.

Avoiding Isn't The Answer

With any type of phobia, a person's first inclination is avoidance. People who are afraid of heights avoid high places. People who are afraid of flying don't travel by plane. Avoidance is the automatic reaction to fear because the immediate reduction in anxiety is an instant relief. But avoidance is not the best long-term answer to the problem. Avoidance lowers your self-esteem. Over time, as you continually avoid situations that are fearful to you, you begin to lose your self-confidence

Avoidance maintains anxiety, even makes it worse, for several reasons. First, avoidance prevents a process called *habituation* from occurring. With habituation, your body becomes accustomed to a certain situation and it learns to not react so strongly. It only takes place with repeated exposure to the feared situation. If you practice avoidance, your body never has a chance to calm down, to learn on a physical level that there isn't a real danger present. Second, avoidance prevents your thought patterns from changing. When you avoid something you fear, you don't learn that you would survive the threat. Faulty thinking patterns keep many people stuck in the anxiety mode. People with S.A.D. make two fundamental mistakes in the way they think about social or performance situations. These are called *probability* and *severity distortions*.

Probability distortions involve overestimating the likelihood that something will go wrong and you will be judged negatively. This type of thinking seems perfectly logical at the time but it's not as likely as you think. Other people have a lot on their minds and may even be worrying about their own performance.

Severity distortions see any instance of being judged or criticized as a major catastrophe. It's natural to want people to like you but even if people disapprove of you, the consequences usually aren't as bad as you have imagined.

Worrying Won't Work

Worry is a major factor for people with S.A.D. and one of the more difficult aspects to conquer. Worrying involves projecting fear into the future so you anticipate and dread something terrible may happen. Worry also keeps your body in a constant state of physical tension. Your neck may feel stiff; you may have more headaches than usual and perhaps you can't sleep well. The increased tension from worry makes it more likely that you'll suffer from the acute physical symptoms of anxiety when the actual feared event takes place. In addition, the constant state of tension leads your thoughts in negative directions.

Mood is a final factor to consider in the social anxiety cycle. You may find you are able to do more things socially and with more comfort than usual when you're in a happy frame of mind. Your good spirits might be because of a sunny day or the approaching weekend. Whatever the reason, you find you're generally more outgoing on days when things are going well.

You will likely find that the reverse is true. When you're feeling down, you may be more likely to hide out in the house and not want to talk to anyone. This is a relatively normal situation unless you suffer from S.A.D. When you are trying to overcome anxiety, the consequences are more severe. When people believe they can only perform socially when all conditions are good, they limit their opportunities. Keep in mind that if you find your gloomy moods outnumber your "up times" you may be suffering from clinical depression. If this is true for you, talk to your doctor right away.

The Attitude Of Acceptance

Acceptance is difficult to explain but it's a necessary and important step in overcoming any psychological problem. Acceptance is a way of looking at ourselves and the world around us. It implies a willingness and openness to see things as they truly are, without judgment. For example, if you're feeling anxious, you're feeling anxious. That's all.

It doesn't mean the anxiety will last forever. It doesn't mean you won't be able to deal with it. It doesn't mean anything except that you're feeling anxious at a particular moment.

We're so busy putting things into categories of "good" or "bad", that we usually miss the actual experience of the moment. All any of us can truly know is what's happening right here, right now.

People think acceptance means approval and this just isn't so. These two things aren't equivalent. Acceptance does not equal approval. For example, accepting the fact that there is poverty and suffering in the world doesn't mean you approve of it.

Acceptance also doesn't mean that you're giving up. It doesn't preclude taking appropriate corrective action. Acceptance is simply paying attention to the way things are and being aware of the problem.

Chapter 14

DEALING WITH DEPRESSION

UNDERSTANDING DEPRESSION FROM an outsiders point of view is unbelievably difficult. Explaining it to someone else when you suffer from it is virtually impossible. Only by experiencing it personally can a person ever truly understand what it involves.

Depression is not anyone's fault. It isn't a 'personality weakness' and it isn't something you can just 'snap out of.' It is a very serious illness the same as any physiological disease except with depression, there never seems to be the possibility that it will end.

Many individuals suffer from depression or manic-depressive illness and function extremely well between episodes of their illness, even when in situations of great pressure, uncertainty, or repeated emotional or financial setbacks.

Depression shatters that capacity. When the mind's flexibility and ability to adapt are undermined by this illness, its defenses are put in jeopardy. Much as a compromised immune system is vulnerable to infection, so too is an unwell mind made assailable by the eventualities of life. The quickness and flexibility of a well mind, a belief or hope that things will eventually sort themselves out – these are the resources lost to a person when the brain is ill.

Clinical depression is caused by a malfunction of the circuitry of the brain. The formation of its pathways and connections are, throughout an individual's life, a product of both inheritance and experiences derived from interactions with life.

In the essence of the brain, its nerve cells (or neurons), communicate with one another electrochemically by sending information out across fibers called axons. These axons branch off into a number of smaller fibers that end in terminals; between terminals are the slight gaps known as synapses, across which messages are sent. Electrical stimulation of a nerve cell causes the release of neurotransmitters such as norepinephrine, glutamate, acetylcholine, dopamine, and serotonin, from storage areas in vesicles located at the end of the neuron. The release of these neurotransmitters into the space between the nerve cells allows the transfer of information from cell to cell.

Neurotransmitters are the lifeblood of the brain, governing the interactions between the cells, brain region to brain region, and brain to body. No one knows how many transmitters there are, nor does anyone fully understand the actions of the more than one hundred identified to date. We are only just learning about the profusion of transmitters that exist, and we have only a tiny notion of their relationships with one another.

Many neurotransmitters and hormones are critical to the regulation of mood and to the activation of the many characteristics involved in a person's actions and behavior. One of the primary transmitters involved in critical and sometimes unreasonable decision making is serotonin.

Serotonin is a chemical found in plants as well as in ancient invertebrate nervous systems and is widespread in the bodies of mammals, including humans. It acts in diverse ways: it controls the diameter of blood vessels, affects pain perception, plays a role in the body's inflammatory responses, and causes platelets to clump. More significantly, from a psychiatric and psychological perspective, it is deeply implicated in the roots of depression, sleep regulation, aggression, and suicide.

We have know for a long time that the neurotransmitters serotonin, norepinephrine, and dopamine are involved with the origins of mood disorders, and we have also known that drugs that have an impact on these transmitters can precipitate or ameliorate depression or mania.

Endorphins are one of our body's many kinds of neurotransmitters. Endogenous (within the body) they are morphinelike substances that occur naturally and are powerful enough to create a narcoticlike high in us when released. The role of endorphins in our bodies has been linked not only with the blocking of pain but with sensations like the feeling of a "thrill" or druglike high.

The strain – the good stress (eustress) – of exercise causes the pituitary gland to increase its production of endorphins in the blood. Researchers believe that vigorous exercise can open up the blood-brain barrier, allowing endorphins in the blood to enter the brain and produce their positive effects.

In the mid-1950s a clinical observation was made. Some patients who were being treated for tuberculosis with a drug called iproniazid became strangely cheerful and animated; despite their grim circumstances and prognoses, they were almost defiantly optimistic. It wasn't long before this drug was pinpointed as the cause of the mood elevation and it became frequently used as an antidepressant. It worked because it inhibited the action of monoamine oxidase, an enzyme that inactivates norepinephrine, serotonin, and dopamine after they have been released at nerve synapses. This inhibition of monoamine oxidase in effect increased the availability of the neurotransmitters. It had become clear to researchers that the availability and distribution of neurotransmitters was critical to the expression and regulation of mood.

Nobel laureate Julius Axelrod discovered that another antidepressant, imipramine (Tofranil), worked by inhibiting the reuptake of neurotransmitters from the synaptic cleft back into the synapse that had first released them, thus increasing their availability.

More recently, the "third-generation antidepressants," drugs that act much more specifically on individual transmitters, have not only radically altered clinical practice by their popularity and use but have also provided further evidence for the role of neurotransmitters in the origins or perpetuation of depression. Classified as selective serotonin reuptake inhibitors (SSRIs), they act primarily by blocking the removal of the serotonin at the synapses. This in turn increases the availability of serotonin in the brain.

Another line of evidence implicates serotonin in irrational, or suicidal behavior. We know from studies of rodents and nonhuman primates that if the availability of serotonin is curtailed or its transmission impeded, animals become more aggressive and impulsive. Studies of serotonin levels and violence are of direct relevance to humans, who share with other group-living primates most of the genes that are involved in violent, aggressive, and impulsive behavior. The impact of serotonin functioning on aggression and social behavior is powerful and life-threatening. There are many lines of evidence to suggest that serotonin functioning in the brain is determined by both genetic and environmental factors.

Neuropsychologists and clinicians have found that depressed people think more slowly, are more easily distracted, tire more quickly in cognitive tasks, and find their memory wanting. Depressed people are more likely to recall negative experiences and failure, as well as to recall words with a depressive nature rather than a positive content.

Some of the symptoms of depression are:

- Sadness, pessimism, dissatisfaction, feelings of worthlessness, hopelessness, and helplessness.

- A complete loss of pleasure in things that used to give you pleasure.

- Sleep difficulties or the desire to sleep all the time.

- Problems with concentration, memory and decision making.

- Lack of energy – fatigue.

- Loss of appetite, or weight gain.

- Nervousness, anxiety, irritability.

- Dizziness or unexplained aches.

- Thoughts of suicide.

The thing about clinical depression is that you can have some rare, good times when you feel relatively normal. But the 'black cloud' can come over you at any time, day or night, and you know that it's always there, waiting for you, able to overtake your life any time it wants to.

Depression can overpower anyone's mind no matter what level of success they have achieved or how emotionally stable they seem to be. The human mind can recall a traumatic event from any point in your life and the thought of it can trigger symptoms that can attack and take control of your every thought and feeling.

In its severest form, depression paralyzes all of the otherwise vital forces that make us human, leaving us instead in a bleak, despairing, desperate, and deadened state. It is a barren, fatiguing, and agitated condition; one without hope or capacity; a world that is "airless and without exits". Life is bloodless, pulseless, and yet present enough to allow a suffocating horror and pain. All bearings are lost; all things are dark and drained of feeling.

Thought, which is as pervasively affected by depression as mood, is morbid and confused. The body is bone-weary; there is no will; everything seems to be too much of an effort and nothing at all seems worth it. Sleep is fragmented, elusive, or all-consuming. Like an unstable gas, exhaustion seeps into every crevice of thought and action.

The horror of profound depression, and the hopelessness that usually accompanies it, is hard to imagine for those who have not experienced them. Because the despair is private, it is resistant to clear and compelling description.

Manic-depression – characterized by episodes of mania in addition to episodes of depression – is less common but nonetheless quite prevalent. Bipolar depression is much more severe, recurs more frequently, and has far more of a genetic component.

It strikes without warning and can last for a few minutes, a few days, or even weeks. When this happens, you must evaluate yourself and your thoughts, try to think around the regrets and sadness you feel and focus on the good parts of your life and the good things you have done to improve the lives of others.

No one in your life will understand how you feel; only you can know the loneliness, desperation, and fear you will have to deal with until the feelings pass; and they will pass. The feeling of hopelessness seems very real and you may adopt the "what's the point of it all" attitude, but give yourself some time and try to release yourself from the thoughts that are controlling your mind. With the passage of time, you will start to feel some happiness with the good things in your life.

The following is quoted from the writings of a man, a friend of mine, who suffered from severe clinical depression. *"I wish I could explain it so someone could understand it. I'm afraid it's something I can't put into words. There's just this heavy, overwhelming despair – dreading everything. Dreading life. Empty inside, to the point of numbness. It's like there's something already dead inside me. My whole being has been pulling back into that void for months.*

Everyone has been so good to me – has tried so hard. I truly wish that I could be different, for the sake of my friends. Hurting the people I care about is the worst of it, and that guilt has been wrestling with the part of me that wanted only to disappear.

But there's some core-level spark of life that just isn't there. Despite what's been said about my having "gotten better lately" – the voice in my head that's driving me crazy is louder than ever. It's way beyond being reached by anyone or anything, it seems. I can't bear it any more. I think there's something that has taken over and I can't fight it anymore. I wish that I could disappear without hurting anyone. I'm sorry."

The awareness of the damage done by severe depression – to the individual and to others – and fears that it may return again play a decisive role in the course of action chosen by the sufferer. There is a terrible loss of dreams and inescapable damage to friends, family, and self. There is also a sense of being only a shadow of one's former self, an unshakable hopelessness; a feeling of failure and shame; and a terrible anxiety that the illness will return.

Everyone has the feelings of sadness from time to time. The differences are only a matter of degree. There is no way to cure clinical depression; the secret to beating it is learning to deal with it and control it without it controlling you. Positive re-enforcement from loved ones and friends goes a long way in dealing with feelings of despair. In some cases, however, love, success, and friendship are not always enough to counter the pain and destructiveness.

No one's life is ever exactly what they want it to be but every day there will be some satisfaction, some pleasure, and some fulfillment, even if it is the result of doing something for someone else. I believe that there is no greater pleasure in life than the pleasure derived from making someone happy.

People seem to be able to bear or tolerate depression as long as there is the belief that things will improve. If that belief cracks or disappears, suicide becomes the option of choice.

The recovery from severe depression or psychosis is a difficult and dangerous time. Here are some recommendations to follow if a friend or family member suffers from a psychotic illness, especially depression.

- Take them seriously.

- Stay calm, but don't underact.

- Listen attentively to them. Maintain eye contact. Use body language such as moving close to the person or holding his or her hand, if appropriate.

- Acknowledge the person's feelings. Be empathetic, not judgmental. Do not relieve the person of responsibility for their actions.

- Reassure. Provide hope. Remind them that there is help available and things will get better.

Chapter 15

UNDERSTANDING MEDICATIONS

THE INFORMATION TO follow is meant to guide you through some of the medication alternatives and make you more informed as to what is available to deal with S.A.D. or, ultimately, depression. It is focused primarily on giving you a general description of medicines commonly prescribed for anxiety or depression, their benefits, and their common side effects.

Selective Serotonin Reuptake Inhibitors (SSRIs)

SSRIs are some of the newer medications used today. They include Prozac (fluoxetine), Livox (fluvoxamine), Zoloft (sertraline), and Paxil (paroxetine).

A medication must undergo extensive testing in large, controlled studies before the Food And Drug Administration allows its use in treating a particular disorder. In reality, physicians use their clinical expertise to determine what medicine is appropriate for a particular patient.

SSRIs have become some of the most prescribed medications in the world due to their effectiveness in treating both depression and anxiety, as well as their general tolerability. They work by increasing the available amount of the neurotransmitter, serotonin, to the brain. The process through which this takes place is a neurochemical chain reaction called "down regulation."

Because this process occurs over a period of several weeks or more, you can't expect immediate results from the SSRIs. Most people notice some improvement in their symptoms after taking an SSRI for about two weeks but a complete recovery usually takes much longer. Some people experience side effects such as jitteriness or agitation, dizziness, drowsiness or insomnia, headaches, nausea, sweating and sexual disfunction. Often, these side effects diminish over the first few weeks of treatment as the body becomes accustomed to the medication.

Advantages

- High success rate in controlling anxiety disorders.

- Easy dosing, often one dose per day.

- Side effects usually mild.

- Non-addictive

- Good antidepressant effect, this being important because of high occurrence of social anxiety resulting in depression.

Disadvantages

- Takes at least two weeks for improvement, often months for full therapeutic effect.

- May need to take for a year or more.

- Sexual dysfunction including low desire and anorgasmia.

- May cause short term memory loss and inhibit the ability to concentrate in some people.

- Abrupt discontinuation can cause withdrawal symptoms.

Monoamine Oxidase Inhibitors (MAOIs)

Similar to SSRIs, the MAOIs work by setting into motion a complex neurochemical process that takes place over many weeks. Unlike the SSRIs which affect primarily serotonin, the MAOIs affect three of the brain's neurotransmitters known as the monoamines; serotonin, norepinephrine, and dopamine. After the neurotransmitters do their job of sending messages between brain cells, they get metabolized by an enzyme called monoamine oxidase. The MAOIs work by blocking the action of this enzyme, leaving more of the neurotransmitter substances available to the brain. Numerous research studies have found the MAOIs including Nardil (phenelzine) and Parnate (tranylcypromine), to be effective in reducing the symptoms of anxiety.

Although these medicines are quite potent, they are frequently not prescribed as a first step because they can cause serious rises in blood pressure when combined with certain foods and other medications. They are also likely to cause significant weight gain.

Foods containing the amino acid tyramine must be completely avoided. These foods include red wine, beer, aged cheese, soy sauce, foods prepared with meat tenderizers, excessive amounts of coffee or chocolate, smoked or pickled foods, yogurt, and sour cream.

Advantages

- Effectiveness in the 65 percent range.
- My be a good option for people who haven't responded to an SSRI

Disadvantages

- Must follow dietary restrictions.

- Side effects can include weight gain.

- Primary care physicians can be reluctant to prescribe.

Benzodiazepines

High-potency benzodiazepines such as Xanax (alprazolam), Ativan (lorazepam), and Klonopin (clonazepam) are another type of medicate to treat anxiety or depression. They enhance the function of GABA, another of the neurotransmitters thought to be important in regulating anxiety. These medicines act quickly, usually within fifteen or twenty minutes. In higher doses they can be used to induce sleep; in lower doses they may reduce anxiety without the sedation effect.

While the quick action is an advantage, benzodiazepines can become addictive over time. This means that your body needs more and more of the medication to experience the same effect, and you're likely to experience physical withdrawal symptoms when you stop taking it. Because of this they are often used for only a relatively short period of time.

Advantages

- Fast-acting relief from anxiety in twenty minutes or so. May feel significantly better in one week.

- Few side effects, drowsiness being the most common.

- Can be taken on an as-needed basis.

Disadvantages

- Potential for abuse.

- Physical tolerance likely with long-term use.

- Abrupt withdrawal after long-term use is dangerous; must be tapered off slowly.

- Can experience "rebound anxiety" when one dose is beginning to wear off and it's nearing time for the next one.

- Very little antidepressant effect.

- Usually not a long-term solution.

Beta-blockers

Beta-blockers, including Inderal (propanolol) and Tenormin (atenolol), are used to target the peripheral physical symptoms such as rapid heart rate, blushing, trembling, and sweating. They work by blocking certain nerve cell receptors; the beta receptors; located within the autonomic nervous system. Their pharmacological action is swift, and people usually notice a reduction in their physical symptoms within forty-five to sixty minutes of taking the medication.

Advantages

- Fast-acting.

- Non addictive.

- Useful for performance anxiety.

- Reduces tremors, rapid heart rate, sweating.

Disadvantages

- Can lower blood pressure.

- Can cause depression in some people.

- Not helpful in cases of generalized social anxiety.

Other Medications

'Two other antidepressants are Effexor (venlafaxine) and Remeron (mirtazapine). These medications are called "combination SSRIs" because they affect the neurotransmitter serotonin, as well as some other neurotransmitters, such as norepinephrine. Because more neurotransmitters are involved, you make experience more side effects with these drugs. Effexor or Remeron are usually tried when someone either does not respond to the other SSRIs or receives only partial symptom relief.

There are other treatments for depression. Some existing drugs have effects on both norepinephrine and serotonin reuptake, while others exert their primary influence on serotonergic neurotransmission. Many new antidepressant medications are under development. The Pharmaceutical Research Manufacturers of America reported that at the beginning of 1999 there were eighty-five psychiatric drugs undergoing studies: twenty-three for Alzheimer's disease, nineteen for substance abuse, eighteen for depression, fifteen for schizophrenia, and ten for other disorders.

St. John's wort, a mild to moderate antidepressant from the yellow-flowered plant *Hypericum*, is currently under study by a large clinical investigation coordinated by Duke University Medical Center. It is widely used as an antidepressant in Europe and more recently in North America. Because it is not considered a drug, its purity and potency are unregulated. Without doubt, it is helpful to some individuals who are depressed, but because it is usually taken without clinical supervision, there are several potential problems. Many people assume that St. John's wort and other herbal treatments are safe simply because they are "natural" substances but there have been instances of rapid mood swings, mania, and suicidal thinking induced by the herb.

Lithium is the most effective, most extensively studied, and best-documented anti-suicide medication now available. It has been used since 1949 to stabilize the dangerous mood swings and erratic behavior associated with manic-depressive illness. Its effectiveness is probably due to its impact on two of the most potent risk factors for suicide: its capacity to enhance the serotonin turnover in the brain (thereby decreasing aggression, agitation, and impulsivity) and its power to decrease or eliminate mania and depression in most people who have manic-depressive illness.

If lithium works so well to prevent recurrences of mania and depression, why isn't everyone who suffers from a major mood disorder taking it? The answer to this reflects the problems, as well as the promise, of psychiatric medications. First, not everyone responds well to lithium. Some who take it respond only partially or, rarely, not at all. Others can't take it for medical reasons, or they find the side effects intolerable. Many others are simply noncompliant; that is, they don not take the medication as prescribed.

Another reason is due to the important advances in medical research. Many new medications are becoming available to treat mood disorders. Anticonvulsant drugs (which were first used to treat epilepsy) are now used to treat manic-depression as well. Then there are the newer antidepressants mentioned in an earlier chapter. The selective serotonin reuptake inhibitors, such as citalopram, fluvoxamine, paroxetine, paroxetine, fluoxetine, and sertraline (Celexa, Luvox, Paxis, Prozac, and Zoloft, respectively), are more easily administered than lithium by general practitioners and psychiatrists. This ease of prescription is largely a good thing, although it makes it more likely that highly effective and relatively inexpensive drugs like lithium will be bypassed for other, better marketed drugs. It also increases the likelihood that the more popular and easier-to-prescribe antidepressants may be given to patients who would benefit more from a mood-stabilizing drug such as lithium and who may actually get worse on antidepressants. Often antidepressants and mood-stabilizing drugs need to be used together in order to obtain the best therapeutic results.

In recent years, advances in psychiatric research have made

the highly profitable marketplace for mood-altering drugs far more competitive. Patients who are unresponsive to lithium or unwilling to take it now have many good alternatives available to them. The most commercially successful of these, valproate (Depakote), an anticonvulsant, has now overtaken lithium as the most widely prescribed, and often the first prescribed, medication for bipolar disorder, or manic-depressive illness. There has also been a great increase in the total number of prescriptions written for depression and bipolar disorder over the course of the past five years which reflects an increase in media and public awareness of effective medical treatment for mood disorders.

There is evidence that the newer antidepressants, the selective serotonin reuptake inhibitors (SSRIs), not only alleviate and prevent depression but also decrease angry, aggressive, and impulsive behaviors. What is unequivocal is that in every investigation of individuals who have committed suicide, researchers have found that depression has been underdiagnosed and antidepressants have been underprescribed. Even when they have been prescribed, they have been given at inadequate dosages or for too short a time for them to take effect.

There have been other difficulties in demonstrating a clear effect of antidepressant medications on patterns of suicidal behavior. There is a high rate of suicide in people with bipolar II disorder, a variant of manic-depressive illness characterized by extended periods of depression and shorter, mild episodes of mania. These people are frequently misdiagnosed as suffering from depression only; this in part because the mild manias are not experienced by the patients as pathological and in part because doctors are inadequately trained to make the differential diagnosis. This can make the illness worse over time. Antidepressants, if prescribed alone, rather than with mood stabilizers such as lithium or the anticonvulsants, can precipitate mania and, occasionally, suicide

More problematically, buying over-the-counter treatments for serious medical conditions such as depression, may give the illusion of treatment and thereby prevent people from seeking out more effective drugs if the depression does not abate. Antipsychotic medications, used ineptly or without adequate medical supervision can cause akathisia (an extremely uncomfortable state of agitation, muscle discomfort, and a difficulty in sitting still).

Some of the reluctance to aggressively encourage psychotherapy in people who suffer from depression or other personality disorders is understandable. Psychotherapy is expensive, difficult, and time-consuming to do and there are conflicts within the psychotherapeutic community about which kinds of therapies are best for which kinds of patients and illnesses.

The bottom line is this. The ability to diagnose psychopathology accurately and to refer patients to colleagues for medication when necessary is a nonnegotiable fundamental of good clinical practice. To do any less is malpractice.

Chapter 16

UNDERSTANDING SUICIDE

SUICIDE, AS AN existential issue, is a major problem for philosophers, writers, and theologians. It is an issue of importance for most of us, no matter what we do or do not believe. Judging whether or not life is or is not worth living amounts to answering the fundamental question of philosophy.

Suicide rates among the elderly are alarmingly high but suicide in the young has at least tripled over the past forty-five years making it one of our most serious public health problems. It is the third leading cause of death in young people in North America and the second for college students.

In 1995, the National College Health Risk Behavior Survey, conducted by The Center for Disease Control and Prevention, found that one in ten college students had seriously considered suicide during the year prior to the survey and most had gone so far as to draw up a plan.

One in five high school students said they had seriously considered suicide during the preceding year and most of them had drawn up a suicide plan. Nearly one student in ten had actually attempted suicide during the one-year period. One of the three suicide attempts was serious enough to require medical attention.

Clearly, there is a difference between reporting the presence of suicidal thoughts or plans and actually attempting suicide. There is also a crucial difference between attempting suicide and actually dying by it. Still, a suicide attempt is the single best predictor of suicide.

Suicide is a particularly awful way to die: the mental suffering leading up to it is usually prolonged and intense. The suffering of the suicidal is private and inexpressible, leaving family members and friends to deal with an almost unfathomable kind of loss, as well as guilt. Suicide carries in its aftermath a level of confusion and devastation that is, for the most part, beyond comprehension.

Death by suicide is almost impossible to define or classify. Death by one's own hand is far too much a final gathering of unknown motives, complex psychologies, and uncertain circumstances and it insinuates itself far too corrosively into the rights, fears and despairs of the living.

Gender plays a role in both suicide attempts and death by suicide. Women in North America are two to three times more likely to attempt suicide than men. Men, on the other hand, are four times as likely to actually kill themselves. Part of the discrepancy may be due to differences in the rates and types of the psychiatric illnesses associated with suicide. Women, for example, are at least twice as likely as men to suffer from depression. Although depression is more common in women, their depressive illnesses are usually less impulsive and violent than those of men. This, in turn, makes women less likely to use violent methods and more likely to use relatively safe means such as poisoning. There is also evidence that men are more likely than women to feel that there is a stigma attached to a "failed" suicide attempt.

There are limits to our understanding of suicidal tendencies. No matter how much we wish to gain some insight to the suicide's psychological world, any light we gain is indirect and insufficient. The privacy of the mind is an impenetrable barrier.

Difficulties in life merely precipitate a suicide, they do not cause it. We know that stress has a profound effect not only on the body's immune system and the production of powerful stress hormones but also on the sleep-wake cycle (which, in turn, play a critical role in the pathophysiology of mania and depression).

Psychological pain or stress alone – however great the loss or disappointment, however profound the shame or rejection – is rarely sufficient cause for suicide. Much of the decision to die is in the construing of events, and most minds, when healthy, do not construe any event as devastating enough to warrant suicide. Stress and pain are relative issues but highly subjective in their experiencing and evaluation.

Sleep loss is probably the strongest element in triggering a manic episode, and mania puts the individual at a very much increased risk for depression, mixed states, and subsequently, suicide. A sharp reduction in sleep - from stress, grief, childbirth, jet lag, work that involves sudden alterations in sleep patterns, acute seasonal changes in light, alcohol or drug abuse – sets in motion powerful biological changes in the brain. Medications such as antidepressants and steroids also induce profound mood changes or provoke agitated and restless states in vulnerable individuals; so, too, can many medical conditions, such as thyroid disorders, myocardial infarctions, postoperative states, hemodialysis, AIDS, head trauma, and stroke. A diet that results in low levels of cholesterol or is deficient in Omega-3 essential fatty acids may also have an impact on the suicide threshold.

There are other major influences on suicide as well. Age is particularly significant. Suicide is rare before the age of twelve. One percent of all suicides occur in the first fifteen years of life, but 25 percent occur in the second.

Daily and seasonal changes also have a profound effect on individuals with manic or clinical depression. Depression tends to be much worse in the morning and then improve as the day wears on. Cognitive impairment, including attention, memory, and concentration, reaction time, and physical strength also show major diurnal fluxes in people with mood disorders.

There is a fairly consistent increase in suicides on Mondays. This has been attributed to the "broken promise" effect, a sense of despair and betrayal when the beginning of a new week, which ought to be a psychological beginning, proves not to be any different from the days preceding it. For others, if severely depressed or disturbed, the tasks of the new week, laid out on a desk or in an appointment book, may prove to be crushing.

The causes of suicide lie, for the most part, in an individual's predisposing temperament and genetic vulnerabilities; in severe psychiatric illness; and in acute psychological stress.

Together, doctors, patients, and their family members can minimize the risk of suicide, but it is a difficult and frustrating task. Its value is obvious, but the ways of achieving it are not. Anyone who suggests that coming back from suicidal despair is a straightforward journey has never taken it.

Many who commit suicide explicitly, and often repeatedly, communicate their intentions to kill themselves to others – to their doctors, family, or friends – before doing so. Many, however, never do; they act on impulse or cloak their plans; they give no chance to themselves or others. But for those who do make clear their desire to die, it is fortunate; it allows at least the possibility of treatment and prevention.

If we knew that suicide was an impulsive, unpremeditated act without well-defined clinical limits, then its prevention would present insurmountable difficulties. The high rate of communication of suicidal ideas indicates that in the majority of instances it is a premeditated act of which the person gives ample warning. Asking an individual directly about suicidal thoughts is an obvious and essential part of its prevention. In addition to a person's stated plans about suicide, there are other major risk factors that need to be evaluated; the presence or absence of severe anxiety or agitation; the pervasiveness, type, and severity of psychopathology; the extent of hopelessness; the presence or absence of a severe sleep disturbance; current alcohol or drug abuse; lack of access to medical and psychological treatment; recent severe causes of stress, such as divorce, job loss, or death in the family; a family history of suicidal or violent behavior; social isolation, or lack of friends and family; and close proximity to a first episode of depression, mania, or schizophrenia.

It is difficult but essential to obtain from a potentially suicidal person an accurate and comprehensive history of violence and impulsivity, because they can create a flashpoint for suicide. Many people, especially women, are reluctant to acknowledge such behaviors; others, for whom violent feelings and relationships are an integral part of their lives, may not realize that their violent behaviors are sufficiently unusual to report them to a doctor or therapist. They also need to disclose a quick or violent temper; how frequently they find themselves in the middle of tempestuous relationships or participants in repeated scenes of verbal abuse, and whether or not they experience frequent irritability or engage in impulsive behaviors, such as bolting from social situations.

There is relatively little a doctor can do to control many of the major stresses in a patient's life: they occur too randomly, and thus are difficult to predict. But there are things that can be done to treat the underlying biological vulnerabilities to suicide, as well as the mental illnesses closely linked to suicidal behavior.

Many children with early signs of manic-depression, or bipolar disorder, are mistakenly diagnosed as suffering from attention deficit disorder with hyperactivity, either because doctors do not recognize the symptoms of manic-depression in children or because they are unduly sensitive to subtle pressures from parents and teachers who feel there is less stigma attached to attention deficit disorder than there is to a major psychiatric illness.

Although there are overlapping symptoms – hyperactivity, distractibility, and irritability, for instance – there are many distinguishing features: bipolar children are more likely to have a family history of bipolar illness or depression, to have mood lability, euphoria, grandiosity, hypersexuality, less need for sleep, and racing thoughts. Their pre-illness social and academic histories tend to be good and their illness is often a sharp departure from their normal level of functioning. The correct diagnoses is important because the primary treatment for attention deficit disorder is stimulant medication, which may aggravate the condition of a child with bipolar disorder.

Chapter 17

DEALING WITH DEATH

ONE OF THE most traumatic events that can happen in your life is the death of a loved one, be it a friend, partner, or child. Death is the great unknown. Once a person ceases to exist on this planet we have no idea or grounds for speculation as to what follows.

There is, however, a potential positive side to this. Since there are absolutely no facts to support any of the "after life" theories, none can be proven or disproved. All we know for sure is that they are no longer in our lives and grieving is a healing process for us. The deceased is gone, and the pain we feel is simply a result of no longer being able to be with them.

The result, of course, is that you can have your own theory of what happens after life ends on this planet. My personal feeling is that there must be something after death. Society and government treat death as the final punishment. The ultimate crime is to cause the death of another person and the ultimate punishment is to have your life taken from you.

I think there is at least as much of a possibility that death may be the final reward and life as we know it is simply a series of tests and challenges. If death is the ultimate punishment, why then do so many good people have their life come to an end.

The scope of the universe, even the little we know of it, is far too vast to allow us to consider that, on earth, we are anything more than a micro-blip in the passage of time. There is so much we don't understand about what we know and so much more that we don't know, that only vanity would allow us to think that we, as the inhabitants of a small planet, are the only intelligent or logical thing in the cosmos. The rational mind must allow for the possibility that there is something worthwhile waiting after the passage of life as we know it.

Don't be afraid to expand your thinking and believe in your own theory of a life after death. It may give you the peace of mind to deal with the unexpected loss of someone you care deeply about.

Chapter 18

SPIRITUALITY, EXISTENTIALISM AND PHILOSOPHY

DEFINING SPIRITUALITY IS a difficult thing to do. The idea of it in many ways defies explanation, making us aware of our own limitations to describe things verbally. Too many people equate spirituality with religion, which is inaccurate. The word "spiritual" is used to refer to an awareness of our connection with all of life and our opening to one another as complete human beings, each one different and each one precious.

Spirituality may or may not involve religion. Traditionally, religion has focused primarily on organized systems of beliefs and involves, to varying degrees, doctrines, creeds, and adherence to rules. Spirituality is more concerned with a "way of being" in the world. In effect, it cuts across different religions, uniting all people in the search for truth and meaning in their lives.

Existentialism

"Existentialism" is a philosophical theory that supports a person's right to exert "free will" regarding the decisions and actions they take in living their own lives.

The life of a flower is predictable – the seed is planted, the flower grows, it flourishes, and dies. With human beings, however, the situation is different. They can make choices, think about their lives and decide what direction they want their lives to take. And they realize they are in a world that does not always make sense, a world that may be filled with uncertainty and where actions based upon the best-laid plans of individuals and societies often have an unintended effect.

The collection of philosophical attitudes that have this kind of view of human existence is called "Existentialism". It is a tendency that has a number of significant themes. These themes have been dealt with by a great number of writers in conflicting and frequently contradictory ways. The fact that these themes are consistently addressed in a significant way makes it possible to include a great diversity of thought under the general term, existentialism.

The chief theme, of course, is existence itself. All living things exist but people exist in a different way. Individuals are able to think about themselves, the world in which they live and they are able to make choices. They can choose because they are free, and the choices they make establish the future into which they project themselves.

Another theme is that of finiteness of our lives. Individuals exist for a short time only. They are caught in what existentialist theologian Karl Barth called the "boundary situation." They come into the world at a specific time and leave it at another specific time. Because the time is limited, there are urgent decisions to be made. People are free to make them on the basis of whatever facts they have available. But the facts themselves are a matter of choice. Individuals select the criteria by which they decide the course of their lives or particular undertakings.

Another major theme is the world itself, specifically what we know about it. A pre-existentialist writer, the novelist Dostoevski, said that the universe does not make sense. There are no underlying patterns that can be perceived by everyone. Life, and the world itself, is often unpredictable and capricious.

All attempts to find or impose an order on the world would fail because no single human mind can adequately perceive all possible facts, make sense of them, and put them into an ordered scheme. If there were such an order or scheme, it would mean that everything would be predetermined as it is for plants. Humans would not have free choice but would be fated to take whatever course was chosen for them.

This inability to comprehend the world is compounded by the individuals' inability the gain a thorough understanding of other people or even themselves. The meanings of their own mental processes, emotions, and motivations are never entirely clear to them as they try to make sense of themselves and the world in which they live. If there is a standard of truth outside themselves, they must select it and commit themselves to it, though they are unable to prove the certainty of such a truth.

Finding Fulfillment

The four "ultimate concerns" you must accept as steps to finding increased fulfillment and joy in your life are Death, Freedom, Isolation, and Meaning.

Death

The first ultimate concern you must face in transforming the nature of your life is the reality of your own finiteness. Some might question the psychological value of focusing on something so dire as the inevitability of your own death but clinical and scientific evidence supports the value of this.

In-depth studies of terminal patients revealed some startling changes in a person's thought process when diagnosed with only a limited time to live. These changes can be summarized as follows:

- A rearrangement of life's priorities. What is trivial emerges as such and can be ignored.

- A sense of liberation takes place: being able to choose not to do things you do not want to do.

- An enhanced sense of living in the immediate present, rather than postponing life until some point in the future.

- A renewed appreciation of the basic treasures of life: the changing seasons, the wind, falling leaves, the stars, and so forth.

- More meaningful communication with loved ones.

- Fewer personal fears, less concern about other people's opinions, greater willingness to take risks.

The truth of the matter is that confronting the idea of death makes us live more fully in the present. We don't know what tomorrow will bring; all we have is today.

Freedom

The second existential concern is the fact of your own freedom. Although this may seem to be simple, you must remember; with freedom comes responsibility. You are the master of your own fate; the good outcomes and the bad. You don't have to dwell on each detail of what happens to you in your life but you are responsible for the attitude you take toward what happens to you.

Isolation

The third concern we must confront is that of our fundamental isolation. Despite our relationships with others, we die alone. There are limits to relationships: no one can save you from pain; no one can provide you with an identity; but herein lies the paradox.

Despite the limitations of relationships, the strength we draw from others can help us face adversity. The fact that we are loving, caring individuals can be a large part of our identity. And the acceptance of our own mortality helps us more fully appreciate the time we have with others.

A Sense Of Meaning

The final existential concern is to discern a sense of meaning and purpose in our lives. In essence, enjoying a sense of meaning and purpose is accomplished by courageously wrestling with the existential concerns of death, freedom, and isolation, and fully participating in your own life. In reality, the meaning of life isn't so much an answer to be found, but a question to be lived. You must find out what matters to you, and then do it.

Philosophy

Philosophy is the study of the ultimate reality, causes, and principles underlying existing and thinking. Philosophy is distinguished from religion in that it deals with speculation rather than faith. It differs from science in that both the natural and the social sciences base their theories on established fact, whereas philosophy also covers areas of inquiry where no such facts are available.

Originally, science as such did not exist and philosophy covered the entire field, but as facts became available and tentative certainties emerged, sciences broke away from metaphysical speculation to pursue their own aims. It was only in the early 20th century that psychology was established as a science apart from philosophy.

Philosophy is divided into several branches:

Metaphysics: which inquires into the nature and ultimate significance of the universe; *Logic*: which is concerned with the laws of valid reasoning; *Epistemology*: which investigates the nature of knowledge and the process of knowing; *Ethics*: which deals with problems of proper conduct;

and *Aesthetics*: which attempts to determine the nature of beauty and the criteria of artistic judgment.

Within metaphysics a division is made according to fundamental principles.

The three major positions are:

Idealism - which maintains that what is real is in the form of thought rather than matter.

Materialism - which considers matter and the motion of matter as the universal reality. Naturalism and positivism are forms of materialism.

Dualism - which gives thought and matter equal status.

Chapter 19

WHEN IT'S OVER

EVERYONE HAS HAD a relationship in their life that ended at one time or another and most of these endings do not happen by mutual agreement. Usually one of the parties involved wants to continue, more often than not for one of a number of reasons.

They may feel so much love for their partner that they can't bear the thought of living without them. Or, they may be afraid to be alone and have become accustomed to the familiarity of the relationship and thus secure.

The reality is when two people are in a relationship and only one of them is happy and satisfied, it's a poor relationship. Life is too short to voluntarily spend any part of it in misery. Everyone should be allowed the opportunity to be happy and pursue unexplored avenues without being made to feel guilty about leaving someone behind.

When you are the partner who wants the relationship to continue and it doesn't, there are ways of dealing with the emotional storm going on in your head. The first thing to remember is that all those feelings of loss and devastation will disappear as time goes by and if you do or say things in the meantime to try and keep someone with you who wants to leave, in all likelihood you will regret them later.

If it's the relationship you want more than the person, you will find someone else eventually. If you truly love the person, your primary concern should be that they are happy and have a good life. If their life with you makes them unhappy, deal with it and let them go. You will feel better about yourself as time goes by and you'll become a better person.

Demonstrating true love and caring is the most unselfish and gratifying thing you can do and what greater sacrifice is there than to let someone you love be free to find happiness in any way they can and without you if it must be.

When you find giving up too difficult, remember these words:

The feelings of love are often selfish.

When we love someone, it's always hard to believe
that our love isn't returned to the same degree.

Sometimes it is; Sometimes it isn't, but it's enough.

But, sometimes love changes. It fades, and we never
understand why. Sometimes there is no reason;
people grow apart; and we never see it happening because we're so encompassed by our own feelings.

When we realize that it might be over, we grieve, and this
is healthy. We miss the other one, and this is natural.

But, we can't make people love us more – and
we can't make ourselves love less.

If they don't love you enough, and you can't change
that, would you want the relationship to continue,
even though they will never feel the way you do.

If you love someone, first and foremost, you want their
life to be good and you want them to be happy.

If you truly love them, let them go if that's
what they need for the moment.

Someday, it may re-kindle, and you may be glad, or you may not.

No matter what age we are, love always finds us again.

Are you a good person?

Good people don't try to be honest;

Good people don't try to be kind;

Good people don't search for love.

When you are truly a good person, honesty and kindness are a part of you and love will always find you.

And then let these next words help you understand the natural
process of healing:

*My life has fallen down around me before, lots of times for lots
of reasons, usually other people, and most of the time I was fortunate enough to have a large piece of that life hit me on the
head and render me numb to the pain and desolation that followed; and I survived; and I lived to love again.*

*But this; this slow erosion from within, is me falling down
around my life, because you're in my life – but not really; and
you're out of my life – but not quite.*

*The fear that I would come home one day and find you gone has
turned into the pain of reality.*

"What will I do if it happens?" I would ask myself.

"What will I do now that it has?"

I knew it was time for us to part; "But Today?"

I knew that I had much pain to go through; "But Tonight?"

*Life is becoming less livable. With each new person I meet I
wonder, "Is this the day that fate has chosen, or is fate what I
have chosen to get me through the day."*

Love is the most creative force in the universe; the memory of loving, the most destructive.

Plans:

Next Month: Find someone new.

This Month: Get over you.

This Week: Get you back.

Today: Survive

And now begins a new morning of a new life without you.

And So? There will be others, much more mine than you ever were; and until then, there is me; and because I treated you well, I like me better.

Research Sources

Daniel Goleman – Ph.D (Author of *Emotional Intelligence*) Bantam Books

Kathryn D. Cramer – Ph.D (Author of *Staying On Top*)Viking Penguin Inc.

Dr. Wayne W. Dyer (Author of *You'll See It When You Believe It & Pulling Your Own Strings*)William Morrow & Company

Jeffrey E. Young – Ph.D (Co-author of *Re-Inventing Your Life*) Dutton Penguin Books

Janet S. Klosko – (Co-Author of *Re-Inventing Your Life*)Dutton Penguin Books

Mary Lynne Heldmann – (President of Heldmann Associates)

Dr. Desmond Morris – (Author of *Intimate Behaviour*)Random House

Dr. Eric Berne – (Author of *Games People Play*)Grove Press Inc.

Michael J. Mahoney – Ph.D (Author of *Human Change Processes*) Harper Collins Books

Dr. James F. Masterson – (Author of *The Search For The Real Self*)MacMillan Inc.

Dr. Gerald Corey – (Professor and Author of *Theory And Practice Of Counselling And Psychotherapy*)Brooks/Cole Publishing

Dr. Norman Boswell – Ph.D (Author of *Successful Living Day By Day*)The MacMillan Company

Barbara Powell – Ph.D (Author of *Good Relationships are Good Medicine*)Rodale Press

Elaine N. Aron – Ph.D (Author of *The Highly Sensitive Person In Love*)Broadway Books, New York

Susan Edwards – Ph.D (Author of *When Men Believe In Love*) Element Books, Rock, Mass.

Barbara G. Markway, Ph.D/Gregory P. Markway, Ph.D, (Co-authors of *Painfully Shy*) Thomas Dunne Books – St. Martins Press, New York

Kay Redfield Jamison, Professor of Psychiatry, Johns Hopkins University School Of Medicine.

Listen With Your Heart

When Will I Learn?

I have learned to never trust anyone completely, for each time I have, my heart was broken.

I have learned to never say too much about myself, for each time I have, my feelings and thoughts have been betrayed.

I have learned to never expect too much from people, for each time I have, I have suffered disappointment.

I have learned to never open my heart completely, for each time I have, it has been stripped bare and left a shattered mess.

I have learned to never love anyone unconditionally, for each time I thought I felt love, it turned out to be a shallow, unrewarding and unrequited emotion.

What have I learned?

I have learned that my emotional life has been a sham, for the lessons I thought I had learned were the result of having never been truly in love.

Trust, Openness, Expectations, Miracles.

I can no longer separate these things for they are essential to true love.

The next time has to be real for if it isn't, then I know nothing and true love simply doesn't exist and if this is so, then all hope is lost.

When true love does exist, then there is hope for everyone and the world is not so bad.

WHEN I LOVE

My heart will be filled with a happiness so wonderful that I am almost afraid.

I will pray that the beautiful joy of the feeling may never grow dim as the years pass but grow more sweet and tender.

I will have a soul mate, a sweetheart, a friend, and a guiding star to light the path away from the impulsive and cruel hearts of others.

I will have someone to help me meet the little misunderstandings and worries of life bravely.

I will have found someone to walk with, hand in hand, through the darkest shadows of life and light them with the sunshine of good and happy times together.

My Promise

I can promise to be kind.
I can promise to be true.
I can promise respect.

I can promise to be near when you need closeness and not so near when you need space.

I can promise to be happy to be with you when we are alone and proud to be with you when we are with others.

I can promise the make your happiness the most important thing in my life.

I cannot promise to be perfect. Imperfections are what make us human.

For This Moment

I sit sometimes at night,
Captured by the cool summer breeze,
Owned, for a moment, by the beauty of the moon,
Seduced by the quiet of the evening.

It seems impossible,
That the turmoil of the day can exist.
That the conflict of human souls can strain the mind and body;
To the point of destruction.

How can there be so much unhappiness in the world?
How can there be so much evil in men's hearts,
In a world that can be so peaceful,
For this moment.

The daily challenge of emotions seems so distant,
One against the other,
Love against hate, understanding against confusion,
Acceptance against frustration.

For this moment, I embrace my emotions.
For this moment I understand my fate.
For this moment I accept my place in life.
For this moment I have the hope for love and need nothing more.

Tomorrow, I will be challenged again.
Tomorrow, I will try to solve the uncertainty and beat back the
frustration.
But, tonight, for this moment I have everything, and it is so clear,
For this moment, I have peace.

My Prayer

May there be no moment in your life when you regret being with me.

May your beautiful eyes be just a little blind to my defects and shortcomings.

May you occasionally make allowances for me, knowing that sometimes, men are just grown up boys.

May you always share in my successes and support me in my failures.

May you understand that sometimes I will declare my feelings too much and too often yet also know that they are always sincere.

And no matter what the future holds, may you be able, from time to time, sit back, close your eyes, and let our time together give you a peace and comfort and fill your heart with a warm glow.

What Is Love?

It is wrong to think that love comes from long companionship or persevering courtship.

Love is the offspring of a spiritual affinity and is created, if not recognized, in a moment.

Love can open your heart and light its corners. It gives you a voice and it gives you tears.

It is the only real freedom that exists because it elevates the spirit and makes the world's problems seem inconsequential.

Love, sometimes draws us back into itself and tries to lend to us the ability to be rational;

It is, after all, not blind, as some might say;

It is, in fact, a radiant light that allows us to see what others cannot.

No Place

My feet have trodden the earth for years,
I've been searching for my place,
I must have a special reason for being here,
I have not yet found it.

I have special talents,
I'm not sure what they are.
There must be something I can make better for someone.
I have not yet found it.

I've touched many lives,
I wanted to believe that I made them better.
I was always searching for a sign that this was so.
I have not yet found it.

My mind was not rooted in my heart,
My soul was not rooted in my body.
I seemed to watch myself from somewhere else.
When I saw myself straying from the proper things, the tender
things, the sensitive things,
I looked for something to warn me that the path was wrong.
I had not yet found it.

And then I found a soul mate.
And my mind and my soul were returned to me.
Then I understood more clearly what I was looking for.
Then I knew the place I needed to be.

From proximity came companionship;
From companionship came respect;
From respect came friendship;
From the friendship came love.

The man who does not see the angels in the beauty of life will be far removed from knowledge and his spirit will be empty of affection.

I see the angels every day and dream of them most nights.

My friendship with you is the greatest gift I have ever received. My love for you is the most sincere gift I can give to you.

The Author lives in a small farming community, has honours diplomas in Psychology, Social Work and Legal Administration. He has 2 sons and 4 grandchildren and has put over 7 years of research and interviews into this, his first literary achievement.